PASTA BASICS

MY COOKING CLASS

PASTA BASICS
82 RECIPES
ILLUSTRATED STEP BY STEP

LAURA ZAVAN
PHOTOGRAPHS BY PIERRE JAVELLE

✳ ✳ ✳

FIREFLY BOOKS

A Firefly Book

Published by Firefly Books Ltd. 2010

First printing

Publisher Cataloging-in-Publication Data (U.S.)
Zavan, Laura.
   Pasta basics : 82 recipes illustrated step by step / Laura Zavan; photographs
by Pierre Javelle.
[256] p. : col. photos. ;   cm.
Includes index.
ISBN-13: 978-1-55407-756-4 (pbk.)
ISBN-10: 1-55407-756-7 (pbk.)
1. Cookery (Pasta). I. Javelle, Pierre. II. Title.
641.822 dc22   TX809.M17.Z38 2010

Library and Archives Canada Cataloguing in Publication
Zavan, Laura
   Pasta basics : 82 recipes illustrated step by step / Laura Zavan.
Includes index.
ISBN-13: 978-1-55407-756-4 (pbk.)
ISBN-10: 1-55407-756-7 (pbk.)
   1. Cookery (Pasta). I. Title.
TX809.M17Z28 2010   641.8'22   C2010-901569-X

Published in the United States by
Firefly Books (U.S.) Inc.
P.O. Box 1338, Ellicott Station
Buffalo, New York 14205

Published in Canada by
Firefly Books Ltd.
66 Leek Crescent
Richmond Hill, Ontario L4B 1H1

Printed in China

FOREWORD

Pasta! A dish Italians can eat every day without getting bored. Indeed, in Italy you learn to appreciate pasta as a baby, watching Mama or your grandmother prepare it, cook it al dente and season it properly.

Pasta represents the *primo piatto*, the dish before the main event. For Italians, pasta is a true dish, indispensable and comforting, a daily pleasure that's available in as many different recipes as there are culinary traditions on the peninsula.

In this book, I am going to try to guide you like *una mama* through 82 recipes and pass on what I've learned from my family and my own eating experiences. Through the photos that show every step and the texts that explain them, I invite you to get started and try my recipes calmly. I recommend that you only take into account the time you have available, the ingredients you have on hand and, in particular, what you would like to eat.

If you don't have a lot of time, I suggest the "express" pastas: the time needed to cook the pasta will be enough to prepare a quick sauce, like carbonara.

If you have a little more time, you'll have many dishes to choose from. I suggest you go to your local market and cook with the ingredients that are in season: prepare mushroom pappardelle or lasagnas in the fall, pasta with asparagus in the spring and a real tomato sauce in the summer. When it comes to homemade ravioli and lasagnas, there's nothing like preparing them with friends. You can prepare extra and freeze some.

Italian cuisine is a simple cuisine that needs good ingredients to be tasty. Finding good products is essential! Be curious and demanding about what you're buying, and find out where products come from and how they were grown or raised. Sometimes, really fresh vegetables from a stand by the road can be better than store-bought organic vegetables, which may have withered and lost a lot of their vitamins. And don't forget about the Internet and mail-order sales.

I would like you to discover the different sides of a dish of pasta, from the simplest to the most complex, from the most common to the most sophisticated . . .

Enjoy, and *buon appetito*!

Laura

CONTENTS

THE BASICS

1

THE BASICS

SAUCES AND PESTO

DRIED HARD WHEAT PASTAS

SHORT PASTAS

1. Mezze millerighe
2. Gemili
3. Organetti
4. Conchiglie (shells)
5. Ruote (wagon wheels)
6. Penne lisce
7. Candele lisce
8. Orecchiette
9. Anellini
10. Penne rigate
11. Candele rigate
12. Gnocchi
13. Lumaconi
14. Pennoni lisci
15. Macaroni
16. Fusilli
17. Paccheri
18. Pennoni rigati
19. Mezzani
20. Fusilli bucati

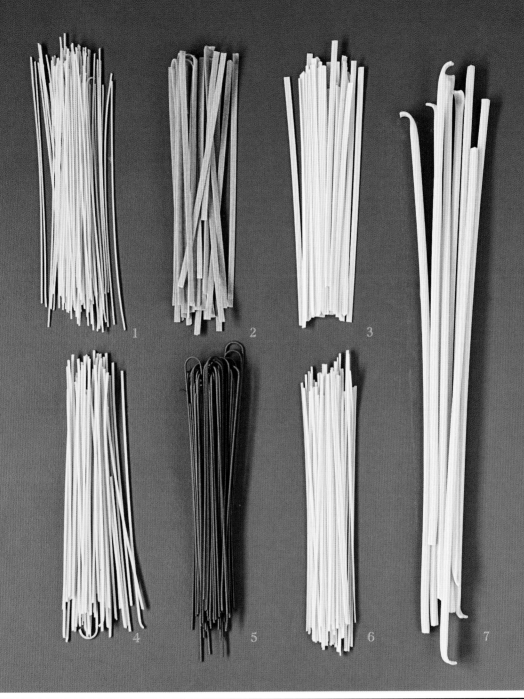

DRIED HARD WHEAT PASTAS

LONG PASTAS
❈

1. Spaghetti
2. Whole wheat tagliatelle
3. Tagliatelle
4. Bucatini

5. Black spaghetti
6. Linguine
7. Ziti

HOMEMADE PASTA

✣ **MAKES: ABOUT 1½ POUNDS (650 G) • PREPARATION: 30 MINUTES • RESTING: 1 TO 2 HOURS** ✣

2½ cups (625 ml) all-purpose flour
2/3 cup (150 ml) semolina
4 medium-sized eggs
Pinch of salt
1 tablespoon (15 ml) olive oil

NOTE:
It is possible to only use flour. However, semolina allows for a firmer texture, and the pasta cooks better.

PRELIMINARY:
To create a uniform mixture, the ingredients must all be at room temperature. Combine the flour and semolina in a bowl and empty onto a work surface.

1 2
3 4

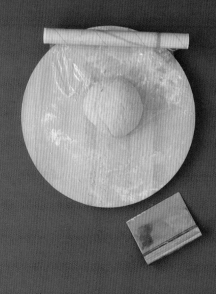

1	Create a well in the center of the flour mixture, and break the eggs into the well. Add the salt and mix into the eggs using a fork.	2	Gradually incorporate the flour mixture into the eggs using the fork. Add the oil.	
3	When the dough begins to come together, use your fingers to incorporate the rest of the flour mixture.	4	Work the dough using the palms of your hands until smooth. Form a ball and wrap in plastic wrap. Allow to rest for 1 to 2 hours.	➤

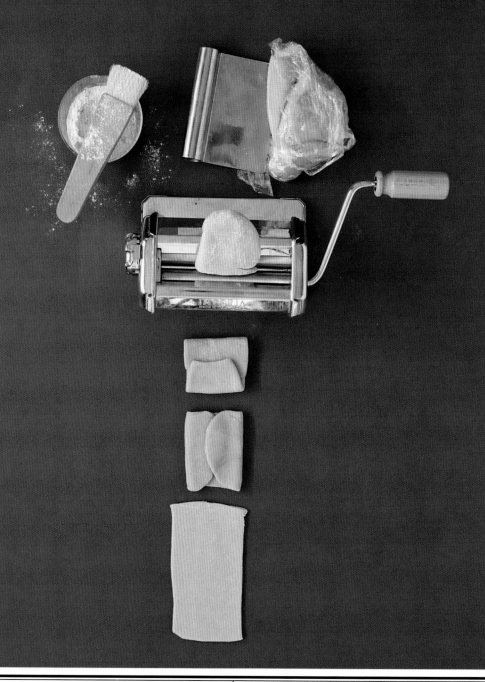

5	TO ROLL OUT THE DOUGH USING A PASTA MACHINE ❋	TO ROLL OUT THE DOUGH BY HAND ❋
	Take about 2 ounces (60 g) of dough and flatten into a disk using the palm of your hand. Flour it lightly and put it through the machine by opening the rollers as far as they will go. Fold the dough over in thirds before putting it through the machine again. Repeat until a fairly regular rectangle is obtained.	Fold the dough in half and put it through the machine several times, gradually tightening the rollers until the pasta is the desired thickness. Cut out depending on the use desired.

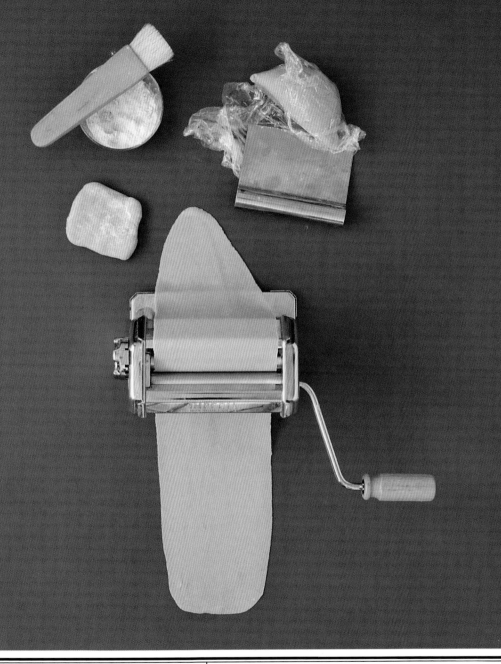

		TIP	
6	Regularly flour your work surface and roll out a portion of dough using a rolling pin, always starting in the center. You'll have to work fairly quickly; otherwise the dough will begin to dry out. The rolled-out dough's thickness will be inconsistent, but the advantage is that it will hold the sauce better.	☞ Continue working with small batches and keep the rest of the dough wrapped in plastic wrap so it doesn't dry out. Flour the work surface often, but remove any excess flour. Use a pastry cutter to easily cut away a section of dough.	➢

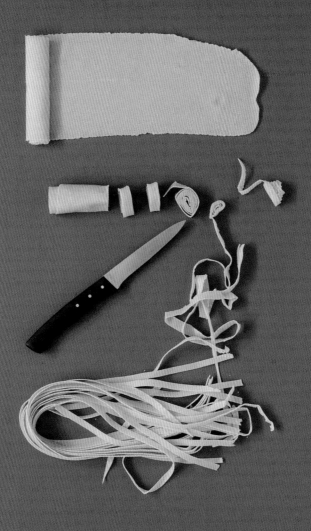

	TAGLIATELLE ✺	**NOTE** ✺
7	Allow the sheets of pasta to dry on a dish towel dusted with flour so the pasta doesn't stick (about 10 minutes). Roll the sheets up, then slice them into sections about ½ inch (1 cm) wide. Unroll the tagliatelle and create a nest on a dish towel placed on a rack. Cover and keep away from any humidity. Cook within 2 days.	Pastas made from eggs and soft wheat flour are typical of northern Italy, where the moist climate helps make them soft and elastic. They are traditionally dressed with butter.

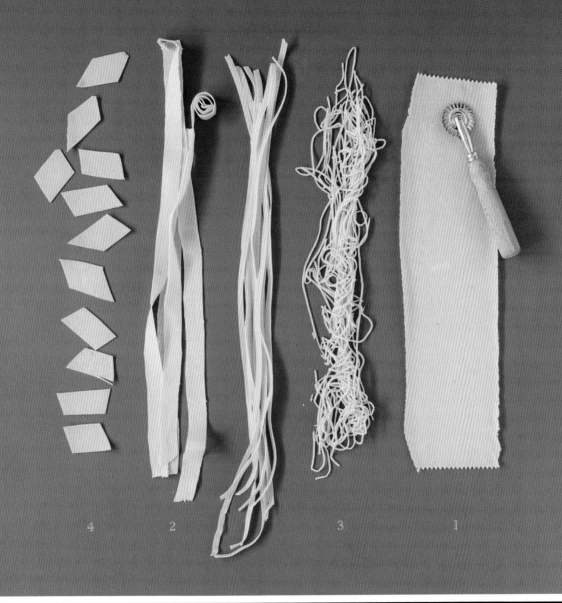

OTHER TYPES OF PASTAS ❈	TIP ❈
1. Using 2 ounces (60 g) of fresh dough, you can make 5 by 16-inch (12 by 40 cm) sheets of lasagna that can be recut depending on the dish. 2. & 3. For pappardelle or taglioni, follow the same steps as for tagliatelle but cut the pieces 1 inch (2 cm) wide and ¼ inch (½ cm) wide, respectively. 4. Maltagliati are cut unevenly using a pastry wheel.	☛ Allow 2 to 3 ounces (60 to 80 g) of egg pasta per person.

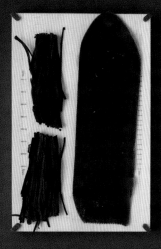

1 2
3 4

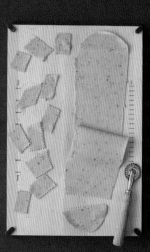

FLAVORED PASTAS

1. BLACK: Dilute 1 teaspoon (5 ml) of squid ink in 2 tablespoons (30 ml) hot water. Beat 2 eggs and 1 egg white together. Mix the squid ink mixture, egg mixture, 2½ cups (625 ml) flour and 1 teaspoon (5 ml) oil.

3. ROSEMARY: : Mix 1¼ cups (310 ml) flour, ⅓ cup (75 ml) hard wheat semolina, 2 eggs, 1 tablespoon (15 ml) chopped fresh rosemary, a pinch of salt and 1 teaspoon (5 ml) olive oil.

2. SPINACH: Beat 1 egg and 1 egg yolk together. Mix the egg mixture with 2½ cups (625 ml) flour, 2½ tablespoons (37 ml) cooked, wrung and chopped spinach, a pinch of salt and 1 teaspoon (5 ml) olive oil.

4. TOMATO: Mix 2 cups (500 ml) flour, ½ cup (125 ml) hard wheat semolina, 2 eggs, 1 egg yolk and 1½ ounces (40 g) sun-dried tomatoes in oil that you have reduced to a puree.

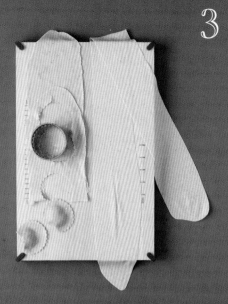

5 6
7 8

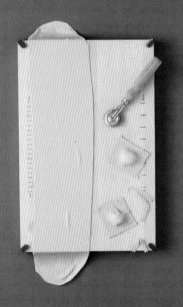

FLAVORED PASTAS

5. CHESTNUT: Mix 1¾ cups (375 ml) flour, ¾ cup (175 ml) chestnut flour, 3 medium-sized eggs, a pinch of salt and 1 teaspoon (5 ml) olive oil.

7. LIGHT WHOLE WHEAT: Mix 2¼ cups (560 ml) organic light whole wheat flour, 3 medium-sized eggs, a pinch of salt and 1 teaspoon (5 ml) olive oil.

6. KAMUT: Mix 2½ cups (625 ml) Kamut flour, 3 eggs, a pinch of salt and 1 teaspoon (5 ml) olive oil.

8. SAFFRON: Dilute 1 teaspoon (5 ml) ground saffron in 3 tablespoons (45 ml) hot water. Beat 2 eggs with 1 egg yolk. Mix the saffron mixture, the egg mixture, 2½ cups (625 ml) flour, a pinch of salt and 1 teaspoon (5 ml) olive oil.

HOW TO COOK PASTAS

⊰ SERVES: 4 • PREPARATION: 2 MINUTES • COOKING: 3 MINUTES (FRESH) TO 12 MINUTES (DRIED) ⊱

1 gallon (4 L) water (1 quart per 3½ ounces of pasta / 1 L per 100 g of pasta) 1½ to 2½ tablespoons (22 to 37 ml) coarse salt, preferably gray (1½ to 2 teaspoons per quart of water / 7 to 10 ml per L of water) 12 to

14 ounces (350 g to 400 g) pasta (organetti)

TIP:
Return the cooked pasta to the heat for 1 minute (except for some recipes) and

combine it with the sauce and a few spoonfuls of the pasta cooking liquid. This keeps the pasta from sticking without using too many fats and helps it absorb the sauce.

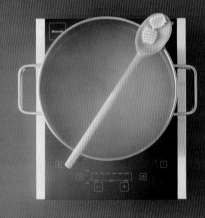

1 2
3 4

1	Fill a large saucepan with cold water, cover and bring to a boil over high heat.	2	Add the salt as soon as the water boils, then add the pasta.
3	Stir often with a wooden spoon (you don't need to add oil). The water should still be boiling. Cook dried pastas 1 to 2 minutes less than the cooking time indicated on the package.	4	Drain the pasta and dress immediately, or the pasta will stick.

TOMATO SAUCE

➤ **SERVES: 6 • PREPARATION: 15 MINUTES • COOKING: 30 MINUTES** ✦

2½ pounds (1.2 kg) ripe plum tomatoes, or
2½ cups (625 ml) canned crushed tomatoes
1 medium onion
1 carrot

1 rib celery
2 tablespoon (30 ml) olive oil
1 bunch fresh basil
Salt, to taste

TIP:
If the sauce is too acidic, add a pinch of sugar.

1 2
3 4

1	Finely chop the onion, carrot and celery. Slice the tomatoes in half and remove the seeds.	2	Cook the chopped vegetables in the olive oil for 5 minutes. Add the tomatoes and half the basil. Season with salt.
3	Bring to a boil, then lower the heat and reduce (20 to 30 minutes), stirring often.	4	Pass the sauce through a food mill or blend in a food processor. Flavor with the rest of the basil. This sauce can be stored for 2 or 3 days in a jar in the refrigerator, covered with a drizzle of olive oil.

QUICK TOMATO SAUCE

❧ SERVES: 4 • PREPARATION: 15 MINUTES • COOKING: 5 TO 10 MINUTES ❧

↝ 1. Peel 1¾ pounds (800 g) ripe plum tomatoes, slice in half, seed, then dice.

↝ 2. In a large frying pan, heat 2 tablespoons (30 ml) olive oil with 2 garlic cloves that you've crushed in their skins.

↝ 3. Add a handful of fresh basil and the tomatoes and reduce over high heat.

↝ 4. If the sauce is too acidic, add a pinch of sugar.

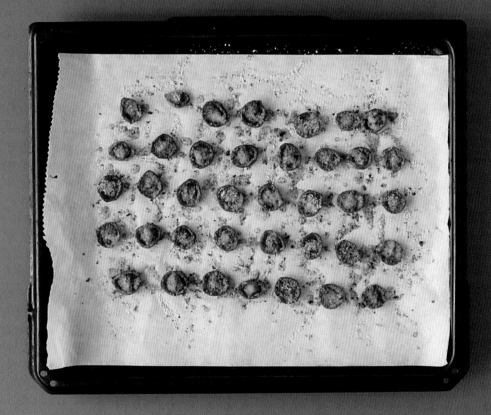

OVEN-ROASTED TOMATOES

✧ SERVES: 4 • PREPARATION: 10 MINUTES • COOKING: 1 HOUR ✧

✧ 1. Slice 9 ounces (250 g) cherry tomatoes (about 20) in half. Arrange on a baking sheet lined with parchment paper.

✧ 2. Dress with a drizzle of olive oil, a sprinkle of salt and pepper, a pinch of sugar and 1 tablespoon (15 ml) bread crumbs combined with 4 pinches of dried oregano.

✧ 3. Place in an oven for 1 hour at 250°F (120°C). The tomatoes can be prepared a day ahead of time. Serve with spaghetti dressed with oil.

BASIL PESTO

⤞ MAKES: ABOUT 1 CUP • PREPARATION: 15 MINUTES • COOKING: NONE ⤝

4 bunches fresh basil
¼ cup (60 ml) pine nuts
1½ tablespoons (22 ml) chopped walnuts
1 garlic clove, de-germed if it has begun to
   sprout, crushed
1 cup (125 ml) olive oil

3 tablespoons (45 ml) freshly grated
Parmesan
2 pinches each fleur de sel and pepper

PRELIMINARY:
Clean the basil leaves using a damp dish
towel or paper towel.

TIP:
Place the blender's glass jar and blade in the
freezer for 1 hour before using or blend the
pesto with 1 ice cube. This way, the sauce
doesn't overheat or lose its flavors.

1 2
3 4

1	Roast the pine nuts in a dry non-stick pan, stirring continuously. Allow to cool.	2	Place the basil leaves in a blender with the roasted pine nuts, walnuts, garlic, salt and pepper.
3	Blend quickly, adding the grated Parmesan and drizzling in the oil.	4	The pesto is ready! Dilute it with a ladle of pasta cooking liquid, without heating the sauce, when ready to serve. Pesto can be stored in the refrigerator for a few days.

HERB PESTO

❧ SERVES: 6 • PREPARATION: 10 MINUTES • COOKING: NONE ❧

❧ 1. Clean 1 bunch basil, 1 bunch parsley, 4 sprigs of mint, 2 sprigs of rosemary and 3 to 4 sprigs of thyme with a damp dish towel or damp paper towel.

❧ 2. Blend the leaves in a blender with 1 garlic clove (de-germed if it has sprouted) and 3 pinches of salt and pepper. Gradually add ½ cup (125 ml) olive oil.

This pesto dresses pasta salads and fish pastas perfectly.

PISTACHIO & ARUGULA PESTO

❧ **SERVES: 6 TO 8** • **PREPARATION: 10 MINUTES** • **COOKING: 5 MINUTES** ❧

❧ 1. Toast 4 ounces (120 g) blanched pistachios in a frying pan, stirring continuously. Allow to cool.

❧ 2. Blend the pistachios with 1¾ ounces (50 g) Parmesan and 1¾ ounces (50 g) arugula. Drizzle in ½ cup (125 ml) olive oil until smooth.

❧ 3. Season with salt and pepper, then flavor with a little grated nutmeg.

MEAT RAGOUT

❧ SERVES: 10 • PREPARATION: 30 MINUTES • COOKING: 1½ TO 2 HOURS ❧

10½ ounces (300 g) ground beef (chuck)
10½ ounces (300 g) ground veal (shoulder)
10½ ounces (300 g) ground pork
3½ ounces (100 g) plain pancetta or bacon
3½ ounces (100 g) carrots (about 1 or 2)
3½ ounces (100 g) onions (about 1 small)

3½ ounces (100 g) celery (about 1 large rib)
¾ cup (175 ml) red wine
¾ cup (175 ml) vegetable stock
2½ cups (625 ml) canned crushed tomatoes
1 bouquet garni (small bunch of thyme,
   rosemary and bay leaf tied with string)

3 tablespoon (45 ml) olive oil
2 cloves
Salt and pepper, to taste
PRELIMINARY:
Finely chop the vegetables. Chop the
pancetta or bacon.

1	Brown the meat and vegetables in the oil over high heat for 20 to 30 minutes, stirring often.	2	Once the mixture starts to stick to the bottom of the saucepan, pour in the wine. Allow the liquid to reduce. Season with salt.
3	Add the stock, herbs and cloves. Cover, lower heat and let simmer. After 30 minutes, add the tomatoes and cook for another 30 to 45 minutes over low heat.	4	Check the seasoning and add pepper to taste. Eat within 2 days or freeze for later use.

BÉCHAMEL SAUCE

❧ **MAKES: 4 CUPS (1 L) • PREPARATION: 20 MINUTES • COOKING: 20 MINUTES** ❧

⅓ cup (75 ml) butter
⅔ cup (150 ml) flour
4 cups (1 L) whole milk
Whole nutmeg
Salt, to taste

TIP:
Add a little more flour for a thicker consistency.

VARIATION:
To prepare a dairy-free béchamel, use 4 cups (1 L) stock or non-dairy milk (rice, soy, quinoa) for every ¾ cup (175 ml) flour and 7 tablespoons (105 ml) olive oil.

1
4

2
5

3
6

1	Melt the butter.	2	Stir in the flour.	3	Once the mixture starts to brown, gradually pour in the milk.
4	Stir continuously to avoid lumps.	5	Cook for 10 minutes and add the salt and 2 good pinches of freshly grated nutmeg.	6	Allow the béchamel to cool; if it's too thick, add a little milk or stock.

2

PENNE WITH TOMATO-BURRATA SAUCE

❖ SERVES: 4 • PREPARATION: 10 MINUTES • COOKING: 10 MINUTES ❖

12 ounces (350 g) penne
2¼ cups (560 ml) traditional tomato sauce
  (see recipe 5)
3¼ pounds (1.5 kg) burrata, at room
  temperature, or 1 pound (500 g) buffalo
  mozzarella

2 tablespoons (30 ml) olive oil
½ bunch fresh basil
Pepper, to taste

PRELIMINARY:
Bring a pot of water to a boil and start
cooking the pasta (see recipe 4).

1 2
3 4

1	Chop the burrata (or mozzarella) into chunks and blend in a food processor. Add a little hot water to obtain a smooth, creamy consistency.	2	In a frying pan, gently heat the tomato sauce.
3	Cover the bottom of 4 dinner plates with the burrata (or mozzarella) cream, a few basil leaves and a little pepper pepper.	4	Drain the pasta once it's cooked al dente, dress with the olive oil and arrange in the middle of the plates. Top with the hot tomato sauce, then garnish with the rest of the basil leaves.

AMATRICIANA BUCATINI

❧ SERVES: 4 • PREPARATION: 20 MINUTES • COOKING: 20 MINUTES ❧

12 ounces (350 g) bucatini (hollow
  spaghetti)
5 ounces (150 g) bacon
5 cups (1.25 L) canned crushed tomatoes
2 large onions

2 small dried chili peppers or 1 teaspoon
  (5 ml) crushed red pepper flakes
4 tablespoons (60 ml) olive oil
1¾ ounces (50 g) pecorino Romano or
  Parmesan

Salt and pepper, to taste

PRELIMINARY:
Bring a pot of water to a boil and start
cooking the pasta (see recipe 4).

1 2
3 4

1	Mince the onions and dried chilies, finely dice the bacon and grate the cheese.	2	Cook the onions and the diced bacon in 2 tablespoons (30 ml) olive oil until golden.
3	Add the crushed tomatoes and chili peppers (or pepper flakes). Cook for 2 minutes over high heat, then lower heat and cook for another 8 to 10 minutes, stirring often. Taste before seasoning with salt.	4	Dress the cooked and drained pasta with the remaining olive oil, the sauce and the cheese. Season with salt and pepper and serve immediately.

PACCHERI PUTTANESCA

SERVES: 4 • PREPARATION: 15 MINUTES • COOKING: 20 MINUTES

12 ounces (350 g) paccheri (large pasta tubes)
5 cups (1.25 L) canned crushed tomatoes
3 anchovies, preferably in brine
3½ ounces (100 g) black olives, pitted
2 tablespoons (30 ml) capers in brine

½ bunch fresh parsley
1 small chili pepper, fresh or dried
1 garlic clove, peeled
5 tablespoons (75 ml) olive oil
Salt and pepper, to taste

PRELIMINARY:
Bring a pot of water to a boil and start cooking the pasta (see recipe 4).

1 2
3 4

1	Rinse the anchovy filets with water. Rinse the capers to remove the salt and chop. Slice the garlic and mince the olives. Chop the chili pepper and the parsley.	2	Melt the anchovy filets over low heat in 2 tablespoons (30 ml) olive oil. Add the garlic, capers and chili pepper. Cook, stirring, for 1 minute.
3	Add the tomatoes and olives. Cook for 2 minutes over high heat, then for 8 to 10 minutes over medium heat. Taste and season with salt as needed, then add 2 tablespoons (30 ml) chopped parsley.	4	Drain the pasta once it's cooked al dente, and dress with the sauce and the rest of the olive oil. Sprinkle the rest of the parsley over and serve hot.

BACON & OLIVE TAGLIATELLE

❖ SERVES: 4 • PREPARATION: 10 MINUTES • COOKING: 10 MINUTES ❖

14 ounces (400 g) dried whole wheat
  tagliatelle
4 ounces (120 g) slab bacon
3½ ounces (100 g) black olives, pitted
1 sprig rosemary

5 ounces (150 g) cherry tomatoes
  (about 12) 18 as shown
1 garlic clove, peeled
1 tablespoon (15 ml) olive oil
Salt and pepper, to taste

PRELIMINARY:
Bring a pot of water to a boil and start
cooking the pasta (see recipe 4).

1

3

4

5

6

1	Chop the rosemary needles and the olives, and slice the tomatoes in half.	2	Slice the bacon into ¼-inch (0.5 cm) thick pieces, and remove part of the salt but not the flavorings. Finely dice.	3	Heat the olive oil and cook the garlic, rosemary and olives over low heat for 1 minute.
4	Add the bacon and cook until translucent.	5	Add the tomatoes and cook for another minute. Remove the garlic.	6	Dress the cooked and drained pasta with the sauce.

SPAGHETTONI CARBONARA

❧ **SERVES: 4** • PREPARATION: 10 MINUTES • COOKING: 10 MINUTES ❧

14 ounces (400 g) spaghettoni (large spaghetti)
7 ounces (200 g) bacon, sliced ¼ inch (0.5 cm) thick
1 whole egg plus 3 egg yolks

⅔ cup (150 ml) freshly grated Parmesan or pecorino, or ⅓ cup (75 ml) of each
1 teaspoon (10 ml) olive oil, plus extra for drizzling
Salt and pepper, taste

PRELIMINARY:
Bring a pot of water to a boil and start cooking the pasta (see recipe 4).

1 2
3 4

1	Finely dice the bacon and brown in a skillet with a drizzle of olive oil, stirring often.	2	In a bowl, emulsify the eggs with ⅔ of the grated cheese and the salt, pepper, 1 teaspoon (10 ml) olive oil and a little of the hot pasta cooking liquid.
3	Add a drizzle of olive oil to the cooked and drained pasta, and mix with the diced bacon over low heat.	4	Pour the pasta into the bowl containing the egg-cheese emulsion. Mix well and sprinkle the rest of the cheese and pepper, to taste, on top. Serve hot.

PISTACHIO & PANCETTA FUSILLI

❧ **SERVES: 4 • PREPARATION: 15 MINUTES • COOKING: 15 MINUTES** ❧

12 ounces (350 g) fusilli
½ cup (125 ml) blanched pistachios,
7 ounces (200 g) pancetta or bacon, sliced
  ¼ inch (0.5 cm) thick

7 ounces (200 g) ricotta, preferably ewe's
  milk (about ⅞ cup/200 ml)
3 tablespoons (45 ml) olive oil
⅓ cup (75 ml) freshly grated Parmesan
Pepper, to taste

PRELIMINARY:
Bring a pot of water to a boil and start cooking the pasta (see recipe 4). Finely chop the pistachios.

1 2
3 4

1	Finely dice the pancetta, discarding the rind. Heat 1 tablespoon (15 ml) olive oil in a frying pan and brown the pancetta.	2	Add ⅔ of the pistachios to the pan with the pancetta and cook for 1 minute over medium heat.
3	Add the ricotta and dilute with a ladle of pasta cooking liquid.	4	Mix the cooked and drained pasta with the sauce. Season with pepper to taste, sprinkle the Parmesan and the remaining pistachios over, and then serve.

SPECK & GORGONZOLA RIGATONI

❧ **SERVES: 4 • PREPARATION: 15 MINUTES • COOKING: 20 MINUTES** ❧

12 ounces (350 g) rigatoni (or other short pasta)
5 ounces (150 g) speck or prosciutto, sliced 1/16 inch (2 mm) thick
5 ounces (150 g) Gorgonzola

¾ cup (175 ml) heavy (36%) cream
¼ cup (60 ml) pine nuts
2 teaspoons (10 ml) butter
Salt and pepper, to taste

PRELIMINARY:
Bring a pot of water to a boil and start cooking the pasta (see recipe 4). Finely dice the Gorgonzola.

1 2
3 4

1	Toast the pine nuts in a dry frying pan, stirring so they don't burn. Set aside.	2	Slice the speck into strips. Melt the butter in a frying pan and cook the speck until it's crispy. Set aside.
3	Reduce the cream by half over low heat. Add the Gorgonzola and stir until it is completely melted.	4	Mix the Gorgonzola sauce with the cooked and drained pasta. Serve with the strips of crispy speck and roasted pine nuts on top.

GARLIC, OIL & CHILI PEPPER SPAGHETTI

⇥ SERVES: 4 • PREPARATION: 10 MINUTES • COOKING: 10 MINUTES ⇤

14 ounces (400 g) spaghetti
2 garlic cloves
7 tablespoons (105 ml) olive oil
2 small dried chili peppers, or 1 teaspoon
  (5 ml) crushed red pepper flakes

1 bunch fresh parsley
Pepper, to taste
1¼ ounces (50 g) pecorino Romano or
  Parmesan (optional)

PRELIMINARY:
Bring a pot of water to a boil and start
cooking the pasta (see recipe 4).

1 2
3 4

1	Peel the garlic cloves, slice in half, de-germ if they have begun to sprout and thinly slice. Chop the parsley.	2	In a frying pan, gently heat the oil with the chili pepper. Add the garlic and gently brown, but be very careful not to burn it!
3	Drain the pasta once it is cooked al dente and add it to the pan. Add the chopped parsley and mix well.	4	Season with pepper to taste and serve hot. Sprinkle the cheese on top, if desired.

RISOTTO-STYLE MACARONI

❧ **SERVES: 4** • **PREPARATION: 10 MINUTES** • **COOKING: 10 MINUTES** ❧

14 ounces (400 g) macaroni (or other
  short pasta)
3½ ounces (100 g) pecorino Romano
4 cups (1 L) chicken stock (or 2 organic
  chicken bouillon cubes)

2 level tablespoons (30 ml) black
  peppercorns
Olive oil, to serve

NOTE:
This version of macaroni *cacio e pepe*
(cheese and pepper) is typical of Rome.

1 2
3 4

1	Precook the pasta for 5 minutes. Drain, return to the saucepan and cover with hot stock. Stir often and add more stock as soon as it's absorbed.	2	Grate the pecorino and coarsely crush the peppercorns with a mortar and pestle (or seal the peppercorns in parchment paper and crush using the bottom of a saucepan).
3	When the pasta is almost cooked, add the cheese and mix well, add a little stock and season with salt, if desired.	4	Remove from the heat, add the crushed peppercorns and drizzle a little olive oil on top. Serve very, very hot.

BOTTARGA SPAGHETTINI

❖ SERVES: 4 • PREPARATION: 10 MINUTES • COOKING: 10 MINUTES ❖

14 ounces (400 g) spaghettini
1 pouch mullet bottarga (sun-dried roe), or
1¾ ounces (50 g) sun-dried tuna bottarga
1 lemon
½ bunch fresh parsley

Pinch of crushed red pepper flakes
1 garlic clove
4 tablespoons (60 ml) olive oil
Pepper, to taste

PRELIMINARY:
Bring a pot of water to a boil and start
cooking the pasta (see recipe 4).

1 2
3 4

1	Zest the lemon and finely chop the parsley. Peel the garlic clove and slice it in half.	2	Cook the garlic, chili pepper flakes and zest in 3 tablespoons (45 ml) olive oil over low heat. Remove from the heat and add half of the parsley. Remove the garlic.
3	Add the cooked and drained pasta to the pan with the chili-zest mixture, drizzle a little extra olive oil over and mix well to combine. Grate half the bottarga over the pasta and mix again.	4	Pour the pasta onto plates, season with pepper, if desired, and sprinkle the remaining bottarga and parsley over.

SOUTHERN SPAGHETTI

✦ SERVES: 4 • PREPARATION: 15 MINUTES • COOKING: 20 MINUTES ✦

14 ounces (400 g) spaghetti
9 ounces (250 g) cherry tomatoes (about 20)
6 tablespoons (90 ml) olive oil
2 garlic cloves, peeled
2 anchovies, preferably in brine

2 tablespoons (30 ml) dried oregano
1½ cups (375 ml) fresh bread crumbs, or
  ¾ cup (175 ml) packaged
Salt and pepper, to taste
1 small bunch fresh basil

PRELIMINARY:
Bring a pot of water to a boil and start cooking the pasta (recipe 4). Slice the cherry tomatoes in half.

1 2
3 4

1	Heat 4 tablespoons (60 ml) oil over low heat with 1 garlic clove and melt the anchovy filets.	2	Add the oregano and bread crumbs, and continue to mix well while cooking over low heat until the crumbs are golden and the oil is absorbed. Be careful that it doesn't burn! Taste and adjust the seasoning.
3	Heat 1 tablespoon (15 ml) oil with the other garlic clove, add the tomatoes and cook for 1 minute, stirring often. Season with salt and pepper, to taste.	4	Drizzle a little olive oil over the cooked and drained pasta, and mix with the anchovy–bread crumb mixture. Serve with the fried cherry tomatoes and torn basil.

SALMON & NORI SPAGHETTI

❧ **SERVES: 4 • PREPARATION: 10 MINUTES • COOKING: 10 MINUTES** ❧

14 ounces (400 g) spelt or Kamut spaghetti
4 sheets nori (paper-thin sheets of seaweed used for sushi), or 2 tablespoons (30 ml) crumbled seaweed
7 to 9 ounces (200 to 250 g) slab smoked salmon

1 lemon
3 tablespoons (45 ml) capers, preferably in brine
1 garlic clove, peeled
2 teaspoons (10 ml) grated ginger
2 tablespoons (30 ml) olive oil

Salt and pepper, to taste

PRELIMINARY:
Bring a pot of water to a boil and start cooking the pasta (recipe 4).

1 2
3 4

1	Quickly heat the nori sheets under the broiler to enhance their flavor, then crumble using your hands.	2	Finely dice the salmon. Zest the lemon. Finely chop the capers. Slice the garlic clove in half, and de-germ it if it has begun to sprout.
3	Heat the olive oil and garlic clove in a frying pan over low heat and add the lemon zest, grated ginger and capers. Mix and cook for 1 minute. Remove from the heat and add the salmon.	4	Mix the cooked and drained pasta with the sauce and the crumbled seaweed.

VEGETABLES

3

TAGLIOLINI PRIMAVERA

❧ SERVES: 4 • PREPARATION: 30 MINUTES • COOKING: 30 MINUTES ❧

7 ounces (200 g) green asparagus (7 to 9 spears)
1 small bunch fresh parsley
2 ounces (60 g) Parmesan
3 green onions
7 ounces (200 g) green peas, shelled
(about ½ cup)

Salt and pepper, to taste
2 zucchini
3 to 4 tablespoons (45 to 60 ml) olive oil
11 ounces (320 g) egg tagliolini or tagliatelle
3 tablespoons (45 ml) butter

PRELIMINARY:
Trim the woody part of the asparagus stems and discard. Cut the asparagus tips and boil for 2 to 3 minutes in salted water. Chop the parsley. Grate the Parmesan.

1 2
3 4

1	Chop one of the green onions. Cook the peas and the chopped onion in a knob of butter, stirring often. Season with salt and then cover with water and cook over low heat.	2	Slice the tender part of the asparagus stems into rounds, and dice the zucchini and the other 2 green onions, including the green part.	
3	Cook each vegetable separately for a few minutes in a frying pan with 1 tablespoon (15 ml) oil per vegetable: they must remain crunchy. Season with salt.	4	Combine all the vegetables, then add the chopped parsley.	➤

5 Cook the taglioni and drain when al dente (see recipe 4), reserving a few tablespoons of the liquid. Add some of the reserved pasta cooking liquid to a saucepan and melt the butter, stirring to combine. Pour the drained pasta into the butter mixture. Add half the grated Parmesan and the vegetables. Add a little extra pasta cooking liquid and mix well.

TIP
✱

☞ Combine the butter and the pasta immediately or the pasta will stick together.

6	Finish cooking the asparagus tips by frying in a knob of butter.	**OVEN VARIATION** ❋ Cook the tagliolini so it is very al dente and dress with the vegetables and 2 cups (500 ml) thin béchamel sauce (see recipe 12). Transfer to a buttered baking dish, sprinkle Parmesan on top and bake in the oven at 350°F (180°C) until the top is well browned.
7	Serve the pasta on plates, sprinkled with the remaining Parmesan and garnished with the asparagus tips.	

PAPPARDELLE & MUSHROOMS

❖ SERVES: 4 • PREPARATION: 30 MINUTES • COOKING: 20 MINUTES ❖

1½ pounds (600 g) woodland mushrooms
  (porcini, chanterelles, etc.)
2 to 4 tablespoons (30 to 60 ml) olive oil
2 garlic cloves
1 fresh sprig rosemary, or 4 pinches dried
  rosemary

11 ounces (320 g) pappardelle
2½ tablespoons (37 ml) butter
1½ ounces (40 g) Parmesan
Salt and pepper, to taste

PRELIMINARY:
Clean the mushrooms, first by scraping
them with a knife to remove any dirt and
then by plunging them twice into clean
water, removing them immediately and
then wiping dry.

1 2
3 4

1	Slice the biggest mushrooms in half or in thirds.	2	In a frying pan, heat 2 tablespoons (30 ml) olive oil, the whole garlic cloves and the rosemary.	
3	In the same frying pan, cook each type of mushroom separately over high heat, stirring, until the water evaporates. Add a little oil each time.	4	Assemble all the mushrooms and simmer together for 2 minutes. Remove the rosemary.	➤

5

Cook the pappardelle and drain when it is al dente (see recipe 4), reserving a little of the liquid. In a saucepan, melt the butter in a few tablespoons of pasta cooking liquid, stirring to combine. Mix in the drained pasta and half the Parmesan. Add the pasta to the butter mixture as soon as possible to keep it from sticking together.

COOKING MUSHROOMS

☛ It's better to cook different types of mushrooms separately since they have different cooking times. Don't forget to add a drizzle of oil and to keep the garlic clove and rosemary sprig in the pan.

| 6 | Combine the pasta with the mushrooms and serve immediately, with the remaining Parmesan. | **RUSTIC VARIATION**
❋
Add 1 beautiful handmade sausage, crumbled and browned.
DELUXE VARIATION
❋
Flavor with truffle sliced into strips. |

ASPARAGUS & ARUGULA STRACCI

❖ SERVES: 4 • PREPARATION: 30 MINUTES • COOKING: 30 MINUTES ❖

1 pound (500 g) green asparagus (about 16
  to 20 spears)
7 ounces (200 g) arugula
2 tablespoons (30 ml) olive oil
¼ cup (60 ml) butter

Salt and pepper, to taste
12 ounces (350 g) stracci (ribbons) or egg
  pasta
⅜ cup (90 ml) freshly grated Parmesan

ADVICE:
You don't need to peel the asparagus, but do
remove the hard, woody part of the stem.

1 2
3 4

1	Cut the tender part of the asparagus into rounds and set the tips aside. Wash the arugula and wring out the excess water.	2	In a frying pan, heat the oil and a knob of butter and cook the asparagus rounds until tender but still a little crunchy. Season with salt and pepper to taste.	
3	Add the arugula, mix through and cook until it wilts. Check the seasoning and adjust as needed. Set aside.	4	Bring a large amount of salted water to a boil, plunge the asparagus tips in for 3 minutes, then drain.	➤

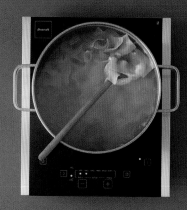

5 6
7 8

5	Cook the asparagus tips in a knob of butter. Set aside.	6	Cook the pasta in the asparagus cooking liquid until it's al dente (see recipe 4).
7	Melt the remaining butter over low heat and emulsify with a little pasta cooking liquid using a whisk.	8	Drain the pasta, reserving a little of the liquid. Return the pasta to the heat and mix with the butter, vegetables, half the Parmesan and the reserved pasta cooking liquid, stirring so everything is well dressed.

9	Sprinkle the remaining Parmesan on top and serve hot.

OPTION
❋

Serve the pasta on a bed of creamy burrata or buffalo mozzarella (see recipe 13).

VARIATION
❋

Replace the asparagus with spring vegetables (such as purple artichokes, green peas, baby zucchini, etc.). To cook, follow the method described in recipe 25.

ALMOND & SWISS CHARD TAGLIATELLE

❧ **SERVES: 4 • PREPARATION: 20 MINUTES • COOKING: 20 MINUTES** ❧

3½ ounces (100 g) dry-roasted almonds
1 handful black olives
6 leaves Swiss chard
14 ounces (400 g) Kamut or spelt tagliatelle

4 tablespoons (60 ml) olive oil
1 garlic clove, peeled
2 teaspoons (10 ml) ground turmeric
¼ cup (60 ml) freshly grated Parmesan

Salt and pepper, to taste

1 2
3 4

1	Chop the almonds and olives.	2	Prepare the chard by separating the white from the green and slicing both into thin strips.	
3	Boil the white sections of the chard in salted water for 5 minutes, then add the green sections and cook for another 3 minutes.	4	Drain the chard using a skimmer and set aside. Add the pasta to the chard cooking liquid and cook.	➤

		FISH VARIATION
		❋
5	Heat half the oil in a frying pan, add the garlic, turmeric, almonds and olives and cook over medium heat for 1 to 2 minutes, stirring to combine. Add the Swiss chard and mix to heat through and dry. Remove the garlic.	This dish can be enhanced with oven-baked mackerel filets; leave out the Parmesan.

6	Drain the pasta and dress with the remaining oil and the chard mixture, adding a little pasta cooking liquid if necessary. Sprinkle Parmesan on top and serve.

OPTION
❋

Add 10½ ounces (300 g) shelled and peeled beans, boiled until tender but still crunchy.

VARIATION
❋

Replace the Swiss chard with a chicory, such as radicchio, and follow the same method

LINGUINE WITH GENOVESE PESTO

✦ SERVES: 4 • PREPARATION: 20 MINUTES • COOKING: 20 MINUTES ✦

1 large potato
7 ounces (200 g) green beans
Salt, to taste
12 ounces (350 g) linguine or trofie

1 jar basil pesto (see recipe 8)
¼ cup (60 ml) roasted pine nuts

PRELIMINARY:
Peel the potato and finely dice it. Clean the green beans and slice them in half.

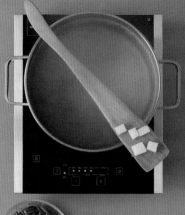

1 2
3 4

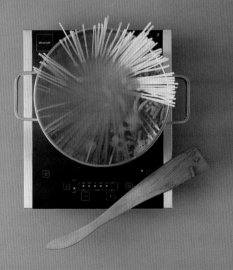

1	Bring a large saucepan of water to a boil, season with salt and add the diced potato.	2	After 10 minutes, add the green beans.
3	After 5 minutes, add the pasta. Stir often.	4	Drain the pasta and vegetables, reserving a little of the cooking liquid to dilute the pesto. Dress with the diluted pesto and sprinkle the roasted pine nuts on top. Serve hot.

PENNONI WITH VEGETABLES

❖ SERVES: 4 • PREPARATION: 30 MINUTES • COOKING: 30 MINUTES ❖

2 medium-sized zucchini
1 red pepper
1 yellow pepper
1 large eggplant

3 garlic cloves, peeled
5 to 6 tablespoons (75 to 90 ml) olive oil
Salt and pepper, to taste

14 ounces (400 g) pennoni or other short
   pasta
6 tablespoons (90 ml) basil pesto (see recipe 8)

1 2
3 4

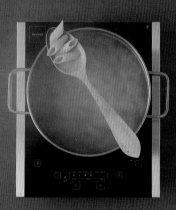

1	Clean and finely dice the vegetables. Slice the garlic cloves in half and de-germ them if they have begun to sprout.	2	Cook each vegetable separately in a frying pan with 1 tablespoon (15 ml) olive oil, 1 of the garlic cloves (to be kept in the pan as each vegetable is cooked and removed after cooking) and a little salt. Stir often.	
3	Once all the vegetables are cooked, return them to the same pan and set aside.	4	Meanwhile, cook the pasta in a large quantity of salted water (see recipe 4).	➤

5

Drain the pasta when it's al dente, reserving a few spoonfuls of the pasta cooking liquid to dilute the pesto. Off the heat, dress the pasta with the diluted pesto and a drizzle of olive oil.

TIP
✳

☛ The success of this dish lies in the way the vegetables are cooked: the zucchini and peppers must be crunchy and the eggplant golden and tender.

6 | Add the vegetables to the pasta, season with pepper and mix to combine. Serve hot or at room temperature as a salad.

VARIATIONS
❈

Instead of basil pesto, you can use pistachio and arugula pesto (see recipe 10) or simply a good olive oil, a few chopped olives and some finely chopped basil.

ORECCHIETTE WITH BROCCOLI

✣ **SERVES: 4 • PREPARATION: 30 MINUTES • COOKING: 20 MINUTES** ✣

¼ cup (60 ml) packaged bread crumbs
1 garlic clove, peeled
2 medium-sized bunches of broccoli
14 ounces (400 g) orecchiette or
  conchiglie

3 anchovy fillets, rinsed to remove salt
Pinch of chili pepper (optional)
¼ cup (60 ml) olive oil
Salt and pepper, to taste

PRELIMINARY:
Toast the bread crumbs in a dry frying pan.
De-germ the garlic if it has begun to sprout
and roughly chop.

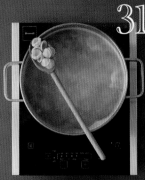

1

4

2

5

3

6

1	Wash the broccoli, remove the florets and slice large florets into 2 or 3 pieces.	2	Boil the broccoli in salted water and remove with a skimmer while still crunchy.	3	Boil the pasta in the broccoli cooking liquid until it is cooked al dente (see recipe 4).
4	Cook the anchovies, garlic and chili pepper in 3 tablespoons (45 ml) oil over low heat until the anchovies are dissolved.	5	Add the broccoli and cook everything for an additional 5 minutes.	6	Drain the pasta and dress it with a drizzle of olive oil, the broccoli mixture and the bread crumbs.

EGGPLANT MACARONI

❖ SERVES: 4 • PREPARATION: 30 MINUTES • COOKING: 20 MINUTES ❖

2 eggplants
Salt, to taste
2 tablespoons (30 ml) olive oil
12 ounces (350 g) macaroni or penne
2¼ cups (560 ml) tomato sauce (see recipes
  5 or 6)

1 handful fresh basil
9 ounces (250 g) fresh ricotta, crumbled
  (about 1 cup/250 ml)
4 cups (1 L) olive oil for frying

PRELIMINARY:
Dice the eggplants into ½-inch (1 cm)
cubes, season with salt and strain over a
bowl for 1 hour with a weight on top. (They
will absorb less oil if prepared this way.)
Wipe off any excess moisture.

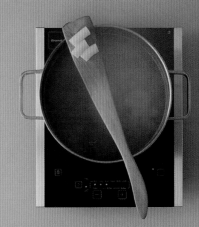

1 2
3 4

1	Heat the oil and brown the eggplant in batches until golden. Drain on paper towels. Season with salt and keep warm.	2	Bring a large pot of salted water to a boil then add the pasta. Stir often and ensure the water stays at a rolling boil (see recipe 4).
3	Meanwhile, heat the tomato sauce and eggplant over low heat. Crumble the basil on top.	4	Drain the pasta and dress with the olive oil and sauce. Serve with the ricotta.

FUSILLI WITH PEPPER SAUCE

❖ SERVES: 4 • PREPARATION: 20 MINUTES • COOKING: 40 MINUTES ❖

2 red peppers
2 yellow peppers
2 red onions
1 garlic clove

3 tablespoons (45 ml) olive oil
1 bunch fresh basil
Salt, to taste
14 ounces (400 g) tomatoes, peeled, or
    19-ounce (540 ml) can whole tomatoes

14 ounces (400 g) fusilli or short pasta

1 2
3 4

1	Seed and coarsely chop the peppers. Mince the onions and the garlic.	2	Heat the olive oil in a saucepan and cook the onions for 2 minutes.	
3	Add the peppers, garlic and half the basil leaves. Cook over medium heat for 5 minutes, stirring often. Season with salt, to taste.	4	Add the tomatoes, bring to a boil and then lower the heat and cook, covered until the peppers are tender (about 35 minutes).	➤

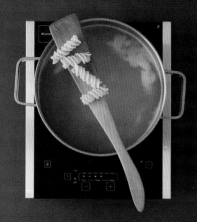

5 | 6
7 | 8

5	Boil the pasta in a large pot of salted water (see recipe 4).	6	Transfer the cooked vegetables to a food mill to remove the pepper skins. If you don't have a food mill, blend in a blender or food processor and then strain to remove the skins.
7	Coarsely chop the remaining basil leaves and add to the sauce. Taste and adjust the seasoning as needed.	8	Drain the pasta and dress with the pepper sauce. Drizzle with olive oil, mix to combine and then return to the heat for 1 minute.

9	Serve immediately!	**OPTION** ⁂ This pasta dish can be accompanied by grated Parmesan, pecorino or good-quality black olives.

GOURMET SUGGESTION
⁂
This dish can be enhanced with steamed jumbo shrimp.

PASTA AU GRATIN

✦ **SERVES: 4** • **PREPARATION: 30 MINUTES** • **COOKING: 30 MINUTES** ✦

14 ounces (400 g) taccole or other large,
  tubular pasta

5 ounces (150 g) cherry tomatoes (about 12)

2¼ cups (560 ml) tomato sauce (see recipe
  5 or 6)

1 cup (250 ml) freshly grated Parmesan

1 bunch fresh basil

6 tablespoons (90 ml) packaged bread
  crumbs

1 pound (500 g) ricotta (about 2 cups/500
  ml), or 1 pound (500 g) mozzarella

2 tablespoons (30 ml) olive oil

Salt and pepper, to taste

PRELIMINARY:

Cook the pasta and drain when it is al dente
(see recipe 4). Slice the cherry tomatoes in
half. Preheat the oven to 350°F (180°C).

1	Combine the cooked pasta and the tomato sauce, half the Parmesan and a few basil leaves.	2	Oil a casserole dish, dust the bottom with bread crumbs and add half the pasta mixture.
3	Sprinkle half of the ricotta and half of the remaining basil on top. Add another layer of pasta, followed by the rest of the ricotta and basil. Sprinkle the cherry tomatoes on top, then add bread crumbs and the remaining Parmesan.	4	Drizzle olive oil on top and bake for 30 minutes. Serve hot. The ricotta can be replaced with 7 ounces (200 g) smoked provola or 3½ ounces (100 g) provolone.

SEAFOOD & FISH

4

SEAFOOD

FISH

SEAFOOD LINGUINE

❖ **SERVES: 4** • **PREPARATION: 40 MINUTES** • **COOKING: 20 MINUTES** ❖

1 small bunch fresh parsley
10½ ounces (300 g) ripe cherry tomatoes
  (about 24)
2¼ pounds (1 kg) assorted seafood, such
  as clams, mussels, squid, fresh or thawed
  shrimps

2 garlic cloves, peeled
4 to 5 tablespoons (60 to 75 ml) olive oil
12 ounces (350 g) linguine
Salt and pepper, to taste

PRELIMINARY:
Chop the parsley and slice the tomatoes in half.
Carefully wash all the seafood under running
water, and de-beard the mussels (i.e., remove
any tough, stringy filaments), if using. Discard
any mussels or clams with open shells that don't
close immediately when tapped.

1 2
3 4

1	Clean the squid and slice into rounds. Remove the heads from the shrimp and take the meat out of the shells.	2	Cook 1 of the garlic cloves, the crushed shrimp heads and half the parsley in half the oil. Add the shellfish (do not add salt because there is salty water in the shellfish).	
3	Cover and cook for 2 minutes over high heat. Shake the saucepan from time to time. Once the shellfish open, remove from the heat.	4	Strain the cooking liquid and discard the shrimp heads. Set aside ¼ of the shellfish. Shuck the rest of the shellfish and keep it in the strained liquid.	➤

5 6
7 8

5	Meanwhile, cook the pasta in a large saucepan of salted water (see recipe 4).	6	Heat the rest of the oil with the other garlic clove and sear the squid until the liquid has evaporated. Season with a little salt and set aside.
7	In the same pan, cook the shrimp over high heat, stirring and adding a little extra oil if needed. Add the tomatoes, salt and the shellfish and their juice.	8	Drain the linguine when it's al dente, and add it and a drizzle of olive oil to the pan with the seafood. Cook for 1 to 2 minutes, adding a little pasta cooking liquid if necessary.

| 9 | Drizzle the pasta with olive oil, sprinkle parsley and pepper on top and serve with the reserved shellfish. | **VARIATION**
❊
Add ⅓ to ½ cup (75 to 125 ml) dry white wine or some lemon zest to the shellfish when cooking.

VARIATION
❊
Vary the seafood depending on what's available in your area. |

CLAM & ZUCCHINI ANELLINI

❧ **SERVES:** 4 • **PREPARATION:** 40 MINUTES • **COOKING:** 20 MINUTES ❧

1¾ pounds (800 g) clams
1 small bunch fresh parsley
10 baby zucchini and their flowers or 4
  small zucchini

3 tablespoons (45 ml) olive oil
2 garlic cloves, peeled
14 ounces (400 g) anellini or spaghetti
Salt and pepper, to taste

PRELIMINARY:
Carefully wash the clams under running water, and de-beard as needed. Dispose of any with open shells that do not close immediate when tapped. Chop the parsley.

1 2
3 4

1	Finely dice the zucchini. Carefully rinse the zucchini flowers and remove the pistil.	2	Heat a drizzle of olive oil with 1 of the garlic cloves and cook the zucchini for 1 minute, stirring. Add the flowers, season with salt and remove from the heat. Slice the flowers in half when cooled.
3	Heat 2 tablespoons (30 ml) olive oil, the other garlic clove and the parsley in a frying pan. Add the clams.	4	Cover and cook over high heat until the shells open (do not salt because the clam water is already salty). ➤

5	Strain the cooking liquid through a fine sieve. Set aside ¼ of the clams in their shells to garnish and shuck the rest.	6	Meanwhile, cook the pasta in a large saucepan of salted water (see recipe 4).
7	Assemble the cooked zucchini, the clams and their juice in the frying pan.	8	Drain the pasta when it is al dente and cook it over high heat in the pan with the clam juice, zucchini and a drizzle of olive oil.

9	Sprinkle the parsley on top, pepper to taste and garnish with the clams in their shells and the halved zucchini flowers. Serve.	**OPTION**
		You can add ¼ to ½ cup (60 to 125 ml) dry white wine and a little dried chili pepper to the clams when cooking.

VARIATION

Replace the zucchini with peeled and diced tomatoes.

FREGULA & SAFFRON MUSSELS

❧ **SERVES: 4 • PREPARATION: 30 MINUTES • COOKING: 20 MINUTES** ❧

2¼ pounds (1 kg) mussels
3 plum tomatoes
2 garlic cloves, peeled
4 tablespoons (60 ml) olive oil

6 sprigs parsley
½ cup (125 ml) dry white wine
2 pinches saffron

12 ounces (350 g) fregula (fegola) or
  spaghetti
Salt and pepper, to taste

1 2
3 4

1	Clean the mussels under running water and scrape to remove the beard, if necessary.	2	Peel and finely dice the tomatoes. Slice the garlic cloves in half and de-germ them if they have begun to sprout.	
3	In a large saucepan, heat 2 tablespoons (30 ml) olive oil along with the garlic and the parsley, add the wine and boil for 1 minute.	4	Add the mussels. Cover and cook over high heat for a few minutes, until the mussels open.	➤

5 6
7 8

5	Shuck the mussels, reserving about 12 in their shells. Using a fine sieve, strain the juice to eliminate any impurities, and then add the saffron.	6	Boil the pasta in salted water for about 10 minutes, until it is cooked al dente (see recipe 4).
7	Cook the diced tomatoes in a drizzle of olive oil for 1 minute. Season with salt and pepper to taste. Add the mussel cooking liquid.	8	Drain the pasta, combine with the mussel liquid and the tomatoes and cook for 1 minute over high heat.

9

Remove from the heat, add the shucked mussels to the pasta and combine carefully. Garnish with the mussels in their shells.

☛ You do not need to add salt to the mussels because they are already salty.

☛ Remove the mussels from the heat as soon as they open so they remain tender and flavorful.

TAGLIATELLE WITH SHRIMP & PORCINI

❖ SERVES: 4 • PREPARATION: 45 MINUTES • COOKING: 30 MINUTES ❖

12 to 16 large shrimps
1 small onion
1 bouquet garni (fresh rosemary, thyme and parsley tied together with string)
¼ cup (60 ml) dry white wine
2 cups (500 ml) water

3 tablespoons (45 ml) olive oil
1 pound (500 g) porcini mushrooms
11 ounces (320 g) egg tagliatelle
1 garlic clove, peeled
1 small bunch fresh parsley
2 tablespoons (30 ml) butter

Salt and freshly ground pepper, to taste

PRELIMINARY:
Chop the parsley and the onion, and crush the garlic. Bring salted water to a boil for the pasta.

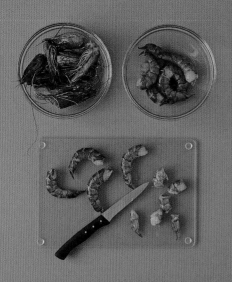

1 2
3 4

1	Shell the shrimp and keep the heads to prepare a fumet (a flavorful reduction). Slice half the shrimp into thirds and keep the others whole as a garnish.	2	Cook the shrimp heads, onion and bouquet garni in a drizzle of oil. Crush the heads with a wooden spoon to extract the liquid. Season with salt.
3	Add the wine, cook for 2 minutes and then add the water. Simmer for 20 minutes.	4	Continue to cook until the mixture has been reduced to 2 ladles of liquid. Strain. ➤

5 6
7 8

5	Fry the whole shrimp for 1 minute in 1 tablespoon (15 ml) oil. Season with salt. Add the sliced shrimp and fry for 1 minute.	6	Clean the porcini by removing any dirt with a brush and a little water; drain on paper towels. Cut into thick slices.
7	Add the pasta to a boiling water. Lightly brown the porcini and garlic in 2 tablespoons (30 ml) oil. Season with salt. Turn the heat off once the porcini are golden and add 1 tablespoon (15 ml) parsley.	8	Heat the shrimp liquid, melt the butter in it, and then add the porcini mixture, the shrimp pieces, the drained pasta and a drizzle of olive oil. Cook for 1 to 2 minutes over high heat, stirring.

9 — Serve the pasta hot with the whole shrimp and the rest of the chopped parsley sprinkled on top. Pepper to taste.

VARIATION
❋

Replace the porcini with green asparagus sliced into rounds (see recipe 25).

QUICK VARIATION
❋

For a quick (yet less tasty) meal, eliminate the fumet (step 4) and replace it with pasta cooking liquid.

TAGLIOLINI WITH CALAMARI

✦ SERVES: 4 • PREPARATION: 15 MINUTES • COOKING: 40 MINUTES ✦

1 small bunch fresh parsley
14 ounces (400 g) ripe plum tomatoes
1 pound (500 g) small squid
4 tablespoons (60 ml) olive oil
1 garlic clove, peeled

1 small dried chili pepper, or ½ teaspoon
  (2 ml) crushed red pepper flakes
½ cup (125 ml) dry white wine
12 ounces (350 g) black tagliolini or
  spaghetti

Salt and pepper, to taste

PRELIMINARY:
Chop the parsley. Peel, seed and chop the
tomatoes.

1 2
3 4

1	Gut the squid, rinse and remove their beaks. Slice the bodies into rounds and keep the tentacles whole.	2	Heat the oil, garlic and pepper flakes in a frying pan. Cook the squid (bodies and tentacles) until the liquid has evaporated. Add the wine and allow it to evaporate.
3	Add the chopped tomatoes, cover and cook over low heat for 20 minutes, or until the squid is tender.	4	Cook the pasta and drain when it's al dente (see recipe 4). Add it, a drizzle of olive oil and a little pasta cooking liquid to the pan with the tomato mixture and cook, stirring, for 2 minutes. Sprinkle the parsley on top and serve.

LINGUINE WITH LANGOUSTINES

❧ **SERVES: 4 • PREPARATION: 30 MINUTES • COOKING: 20 MINUTES** ❧

1¾ pounds (800 g) whole langoustines
  (scampi)
14 ounces (400 g) linguine or spaghetti
1 onion
1 garlic clove, peeled
1 small bunch flat-leaf parsley

1 or 2 dried chili peppers, or ½ to 1 teaspoon
  (2 to 5 ml) crushed red pepper flakes
¼ cup (60 ml) olive oil
½ cup (125 ml) dry white wine
2¾ cup (675 ml) tomato sauce
2 tablespoons (30 ml) bread crumbs

Salt and ground pepper, to taste

PRELIMINARY:
Wash the langoustines to remove the sand.
Cook the pasta so it's al dente (see recipe 4).
Mince the onion and slice the garlic in half.
Chop the parsley.

1 2
3 4

1	Using a pair of scissors, slit open the langoustines' ventral carapace (the shell along their stomachs).	2	Lightly brown the minced onion, garlic and chili pepper in the olive oil.	
3	Add the langoustines (scampi), cook for 2 minutes and then add the wine. Allow the liquid to evaporate.	4	Add the tomato sauce, half the parsley and the bread crumbs. Bring to a boil, then thicken the sauce over medium heat.	➤

Remove the langoustines and set aside. Drain the pasta and add it, a drizzle of oil and a little pasta cooking liquid to the sauce. Cook for 1 minute.

VARIATION
❊

Scampi in busara, a popular dish in Venice. Add 1 cup (250 ml) dry white wine instead of the tomato sauce, allow it to reduce and then sprinkle with the bread crumbs and chopped parsley.

6	Serve with the langoustines and sprinkle with the parsley and pepper to taste.

PRODUCT INFO
※

The best langoustines (scampi) are caught in the spring. Choose ones that have their head and their legs still attached, a shiny carapace and eyes that are black and bright. They should smell pleasant. Eat as soon as possible after buying.

BUCATINI WITH SARDINES

✦ **SERVES: 4 • PREPARATION: 30 MINUTES • COOKING: 50 MINUTES** ✦

¼ cup (60 ml) raisins
1 medium onion
3 teaspoons (15 ml) fennel seeds
10 to 12 fresh sardines, plus 4 to garnish
4 tablespoons (60 ml) olive oil
1 sachet ground saffron

3 tablespoons (45 ml) pine nuts
2 anchovies, rinsed to remove the salt, or 2 teaspoons (10 ml) anchovy paste
12 ounces (350 g) bucatini (long, hollow spaghetti)
1 fennel bulb

Salt and ground pepper, to taste

PRELIMINARY:
Soak the raisins for 15 minutes in a bowl of warm water. Finely chop the onion.

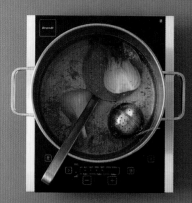

1 2
3 4

1	Bring 2 quarts (2 L) water to a boil and add the fennel seeds in a tea egg (or wrapped in cheesecloth) and the fennel bulb. Season with salt. Cook for 15 minutes. Strain the cooking liquid, reserve the liquid and discard the fennel.	2	Clean the sardines by removing the scales with a paper towel and cutting off the heads and gutting them. Starting at the tail, grab the spine between 2 fingers and separate the flesh to make 2 fillets.	
3	Lightly brown the onion for 2 minutes in 1 tablespoon (15 ml) oil, then add a glass of the fennel cooking liquid. Reduce by half.	4	Add 3 tablespoons (45 ml) oil, the saffron, the raisins and the pine nuts. Simmer for 5 minutes.	➢

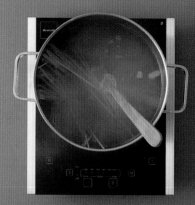

5 6
7 8

5	Add the chopped anchovies, cook until melted and then add the sardines (except those set aside to garnish). Lightly season with salt and pepper, and cook for another 5 minutes over low heat.	6	Bring the rest of the fennel cooking liquid and 2 quarts (2 L) water to a boil, season with salt and cook the pasta (see recipe 4).
7	Fry the remaining sardines in a drizzle of oil for 2 minutes or deep fry.	8	Drain the pasta when it's al dente and dress with a drizzle of oil and the sardine sauce.

9 Garnish each plate of pasta with the fried or deep-fried sardines. Serve.

OVEN VARIATION
❋

This pasta is excellent prepared in the oven. Prepare the sauce using all the sardines, cook the pasta so it's very al dente, and then drain it and dress it generously with oil. In an oiled casserole dish, alternate layers of pasta and sauce, and finish with a layer of sauce, bread crumbs and pine nuts. Bake in the oven. Serve hot or cold.

SPAGHETTI WITH FRESH TUNA

❖ SERVES: 4 • PREPARATION: 30 MINUTES • COOKING: 20 MINUTES ❖

7 ounces (200 g) ripe cherry tomatoes (about 15)
1 small bunch fresh parsley
1 small bunch fresh basil

2 tablespoons (30 ml) black olives
2 garlic cloves, peeled
2 tablespoons (30 ml) capers in brine
10½ ounces (300 g) fresh tuna

4 tablespoons (60 ml) olive oil
14 ounces (400 g) spaghetti
Salt and pepper, to taste

1 2
3 4

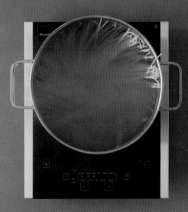

1	Slice the tomatoes in half, chop the parsley, basil and olives and slice the garlic in half. Strain the capers, rinse under water (to remove salt) and chop. Dice the tuna.	2	In a frying pan, heat 3 tablespoons (45 ml) oil and cook the garlic, capers and olives. Add the tomatoes and cook for 1 minute, stirring. Set aside.
3	In the same pan, cook the tuna for 2 minutes over high heat with 1 tablespoon (15 ml) olive oil, stirring. Season with salt and pepper. Set aside.	4	Meanwhile, bring a large saucepan of salted water to a boil and cook the pasta (see recipe 4). ➢

| 5 | Drain the pasta when it's al dente and add it, a drizzle of olive oil, the herbs (reserving a little as a garnish) and a little pasta cooking liquid to the pan with the tomatoes. Stir until well combined. Remove the garlic. | **VARIATION**
❋

Replace the tuna with swordfish and the fresh tomatoes with oven-roasted tomatoes (see recipe 7), which are added at the end. |

6	Sprinkle the rest of the herbs on top and serve with the diced tuna.

PRODUCT INFO
❋

Avoid buying bluefin tuna from the Mediterranean because it is threatened with extinction.

ADVICE
❋

☛ The tuna must remain pink in the middle or it will be too dry.

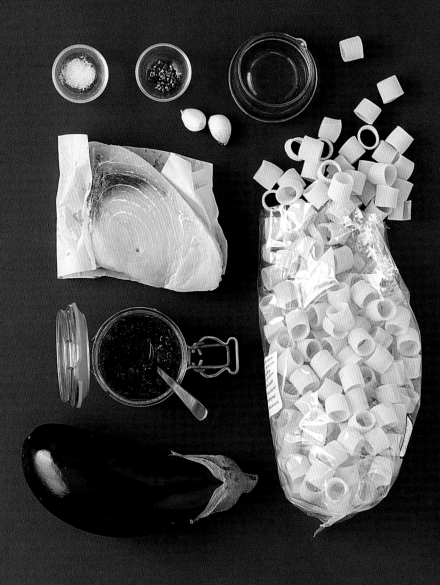

MEZZE MANICHE WITH SWORDFISH

❧ **SERVES: 4 • PREPARATION: 30 MINUTES • COOKING: 30 MINUTES** ❧

1 large eggplant
¼ cup (60 ml) olive oil
2 garlic cloves, peeled
14 ounces (400 g) mezze maniche or other
   short pasta

10½ ounces (300 g) fresh sliced swordfish
2 tablespoons (30 ml) herb pesto (see recipe 9)
Salt and ground pepper, to taste

PRELIMINARY:
Dice the eggplant.

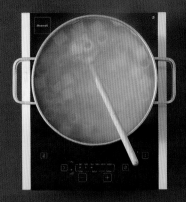

1 2
3 4

1	Brown the eggplant in 2 batches with 1 tablespoon (15 ml) olive oil and 1 of the garlic cloves until golden and tender. Season with salt.	2	Bring a large pot of water to a boil, season with salt and cook the pasta (see recipe 4).
3	Cut the swordfish into about a ¾-inch (2 cm) dice. Cook for 1 minute over high heat in 2 tablespoons (30 ml) oil. Season with salt and pepper.	4	Drain the pasta when it's al dente and dress with a drizzle of oil, the pesto and a few spoonfuls of pasta cooking liquid. Add the diced eggplant and swordfish. Serve.

PISTACHIO & BOTTARGA GNOCCHI

➤ **SERVES: 4 • PREPARATION: 20 MINUTES • COOKING: 20 MINUTES** ◄

14 ounces 400 g dried gnocchi (hard wheat
  pasta)
3½ ounces (100 g) blanched pistachios
Olive oil
Salt and pepper, to taste

2 pinches crushed red pepper flakes
1 bunch fresh parsley
1¾ ounces (50 g) tuna bottarga (dried or
  in oil)

PRELIMINARY:
Toast the pistachios in a 325°F (160°C)
oven for 10 minutes at or in a dry skillet,
stirring constantly. Allow to cool.

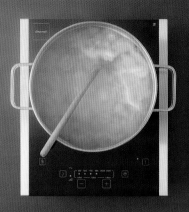

1 2
3 4

1	Bring a large pot of salted water to a boil and cook the pasta (see recipe 4).	2	Blend the pistachios in a food processor or blender, adding the olive oil in a drizzle until a paste is obtained. Season with salt, pepper and the red pepper flakes.
3	Chop the parsley, and drain and crumble the bottarga if it is in oil or grate it if it is dried. Blend with the pistachio mixture.	4	Drain the pasta when it's al dente and dress it with the pistachio-bottarga pesto, diluted with 1 ladle of pasta cooking liquid.

ONION & ANCHOVY SPAGHETTONI

❖ **SERVES:** 4 • PREPARATION: 15 MINUTES • COOKING: 40 MINUTES ❖

1¾ pounds (800 g) sweet onions
1 tablespoon (15 ml) parsley (optional)
3 ounces (80 g) anchovies in brine
½ cup (125 ml) olive oil

14 ounces (400 g) whole wheat spaghettoni
2 tablespoons (30 ml) toasted bread crumbs
Salt and pepper, to taste

PRELIMINARY:
Slice the onion (can be done in a food processor). Chop the parsley.

1 2
3 4

1	Quickly rinse the anchovies under running water to remove the salt. Clean, remove the spine and roughly chop.	2	Heat the oil in a saucepan and add the anchovies, then the onions. Cover and lower the heat. Cook until the onions have softened, about 40 minutes. Add a little water as needed.
3	Meanwhile, cook the pasta and drain when it's al dente (see recipe 4). Add the drained pasta to the sauce and combine.	4	Sprinkle the parsley and bread crumbs on top, and season with pepper. Serve in shallow bowls with the anchovies arranged on top.

MEATS

5

TAGLIATELLE WITH DUCK

❖ **SERVES: 4 • PREPARATION: 15 MINUTES • COOKING: 20 MINUTES** ❖

1½ ounces (40 g) Parmesan
2 leeks
1 onion
2 ribs celery
1 carrot

10½ ounces (300 g) duck aiguillettes (duck fillets)
4 tablespoons (60 ml) olive oil
1 sprig rosemary
6 cups (1.2 L) chicken stock

12 ounces (350 g) egg & rosemary tagliatelle (see recipe 3)
2½ tablespoons (37 ml) butter
Salt and pepper, to taste
PRELIMINARY:
Grate the Parmesan.

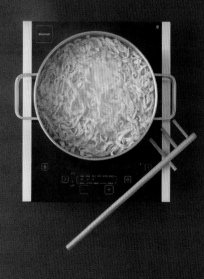

1	Wash, peel and finely chop the vegetables. Finely dice the duck.	2	Cook the vegetables for 3 minutes in half the olive oil. Season with salt.	
3	Cook the duck for 2 minutes over high heat in the other half of the olive oil and the rosemary. Season with salt.	4	Bring half the chicken stock to a boil, add the pasta and stir.	➤

	Add the cooked vegetables and the duck to the pasta, then gradually add hot chicken stock, mixing as you would when making a risotto.	**COOKING INFO** ❊ Cook the pasta in the stock until enough liquid is absorbed and a creamy sauce is obtained, as with a risotto.
5		

6 Finish cooking by allowing all the liquid to be absorbed. Remove from the heat, add the butter and ¾ of the Parmesan. Mix well, sprinkle the rest of the Parmesan on top and serve.	**VARIATION** ❋ Replace the duck with another fowl and vary the vegetables according to the season (green peas, asparagus, zucchini, etc.).

TAGLIOLINI WITH VEAL AND GREEN PEAS

⇾ SERVES: 4 • PREPARATION: 30 MINUTES • COOKING: 40 MINUTES ⇽

1¾ ounces (50 g) dried porcini mushrooms
1¾ ounces (50 g) Parmesan
2 shallots
1 carrot
1 rib celery
3 tablespoons (45 ml) olive oil
14 ounces (400 g) veal shoulder, chopped

¼ cup (60 ml) dry white wine
1½ to 2 cups (375 to 500 ml) vegetable stock
1 bouquet garni (fresh rosemary, thyme and a
  bay leaf tied with string)
7 ounces (200 g) green peas, shelled (about
  ½ cup/125 ml)

10½ ounces (300 g) egg tagliolini (see recipe 2)
2½ tablespoons (37 ml) butter
Salt and pepper, to taste
PRELIMINARY:
Soak the dried mushrooms in a bowl of warm
water for 20 minutes. Grate the Parmesan.

1	Peel, then mince the vegetables. Dry the re-hydrated porcini mushrooms on paper towels, then chop.	2	Over high heat, lightly brown all the vegetables except the green peas for 2 minutes in the oil, then add the meat and mix well.
3	When the meat starts to stick to the bottom of the pan, add the wine and allow it to reduce. Season with salt.	4	Moisten with the vegetable stock, add the bouquet garni, cover and simmer for 30 minutes. ➤

5	Cook the green peas over low heat in a little salted water (or a little stock) until tender.	6	Add the green peas to the meat mixture, then remove the bouquet garni.
7	Boil the pasta in salted water (see recipe 04). Drain when it's al dente, reserving 1 ladle of cooking liquid.	8	Mix the cooking liquid and the butter until creamy. Add the pasta, mix to combine and then add half of the Parmesan.

9

Serve the pasta with the ragout and sprinkle the remaining Parmesan on top.

VARIATION
❋

The veal can be replaced with a mixture of beef, pork and veal, or with meat ragout (see recipe 11).

PRODUCT ADVICE
❋

☛ In season, use fresh porcini mushrooms or chanterelles (see recipe 26 for how to cook).

LAMB MALTAGLIATI

❖ SERVES: 4 • PREPARATION: 30 MINUTES • COOKING: 45 MINUTES ❖

4 baby artichoke hearts, fresh or frozen
4 tablespoons (60 ml) olive oil
2 garlic cloves, peeled
14 ounces (400 g) lamb shoulder, fat removed and meat finely diced

½ cup (125 ml) dry white wine
11 ounces (320 g) tomato maltagliati (see recipe 3)
Salt and pepper, to taste

¾ cup (175 ml vegetable stock
1 bay leaf
¼ cup (60 ml) butter
⅔ cup (150 ml) grated Parmesan

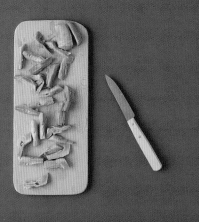

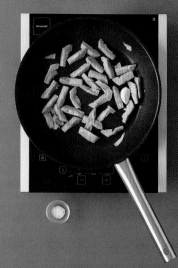

1 2
3 4

1	Slice the artichoke hearts into quarters.	2	Fry the artichoke hearts in half the olive oil with 1 of the garlic cloves for 2 to 3 minutes. Season with salt.	
3	Heat the remaining oil with the other garlic clove and add the meat. Brown over high heat until golden. Add in the wine and allow it to reduce. Season with salt and pepper.	4	Add the artichokes, the vegetable stock and the bay leaf, and mix to combine. Ccover and simmer for 30 minutes.	➤

5	Boil the pasta in salted water (see recipe 4). In a bowl, melt the butter with ½ ladle pasta cooking liquid. Drain the pasta and combine with the melted butter and half the Parmesan.	**PRODUCT INFO** ❋ Maltagliatie (literally "badly cut") are irregularly shaped pasta. They can be replaced with tagliatelle.

Serve the pasta with the artichoke and lamb sauce. Season with pepper and sprinkle the remaining Parmesan on top.

VARIATION
❃

Lamb is a typical dish in central and southern Italy. The artichokes can be replaced with red peppers and peeled tomatoes.

MALLOREDDUS WITH SAUSAGE

⟡ SERVES: 4 • PREPARATION: 15 MINUTES • COOKING: 30 MINUTES ⟡

1 large onion
1 garlic clove, peeled
½ bunch fresh parsley
9 ounces (250 g) fresh pork sausage
1 teaspoon (5 ml) fennel seeds

1¾ ounces (50 g) pecorino Sardo or
   Romano (or Parmesan)
2 tablespoons (30 ml) olive oil
⅓ cup (75 ml) white wine
4½ cup (4.125 L) crushed tomatoes, fresh

   or canned
1 pinch crushed red pepper flakes
14 ounces (400 g) malloreddus (Sardinian
   gnocchetti)
Salt and pepper, to taste

1 2
3 4

1	Peel and chop the onion and the garlic (de-germ it if it has begun to sprout). Chop the parsley. Remove the casing from the sausages and crumble the meat. Crush the fennel seeds. Grate the pecorino.	2	Lightly brown the onion in the olive oil for 2 minutes, and then add the garlic and the sausage. Brown the meat well, then add the white wine and reduce the liquid by half.
3	Add the crushed fennel seeds, tomatoes, red pepper flakes, season with salt and cook over low heat, half covered, for 20 to 30 minutes.	4	Meanwhile, cook the pasta (see recipe 4). Drain and dress it with the sauce, parsley and pepper. Sprinkle the grated pecorino on top.

SAUSAGE & LEEK PENNE

❖ SERVES: 4 • PREPARATION: 15 MINUTES • COOKING: 30 MINUTES ❖

14 ounces (400 g) spelt or Kamut penne
2½ ounces (70 g) Parmigiano-Reggiano
10½ ounces (300 g) leeks

2 tablespoons (30 ml) olive oil
10½ to 14 ounces (300 to 400 g) fresh pork
   sausage

½ cup (125 ml) dry white wine
Salt and pepper, to taste

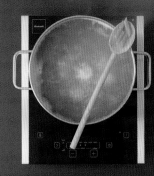

1
2
3

4
5
6

1	Bring a large pot of water to a boil. Add salt and then add the pasta.	2	Grate the Parmigiano-Reggiano. Wash and finely chop the leeks.	3	Cook in the oil over medium heat for 3 minutes, stirring often.
4	Slit open the sausages to remove the casing and crumble the meat using a fork.	5	Add the sausage to the leeks and brown. Add the wine and allow it to reduce. Season with salt and pepper.	6	Drain the pasta and add a little of the cooking liquid. Sprinkle the Parmigiano-Reggiano and a little pepper on top.

LUMACONI AU GRATIN

✦ SERVES: 4 • PREPARATION: 30 MINUTES • COOKING: 20 MINUTES ✦

7 ounces (200 g) fresh porcini, cooked
  (see recipe 26)
1 shallot
5 ounces (150 g) cooked ham
3½ ounces (100 g) Parmesan
1 tablespoon (15 ml) olive oil

5 ounces (150 g) ricotta (about ⅔ cup/
  150 ml)
5 ounces (150 g) mascarpone
  (about ⅔ cup/150 ml)
1 egg
¼ cup (60 ml) heavy cream (36%)

Salt and pepper, to taste
9 ounces (250 g) lumaconi or conchiglioni
2 tablespoons (30 ml) butter

1	Dice the porcini, and peel and mince the shallot. Finely chop the ham. Grate the Parmesan. Preheat the oven to 350°F (180°C).	2	Cook the shallot for 5 minutes over low heat in the olive oil. Season with salt. Remove from the heat and mix with the cooked mushrooms.
3	Mix the ham, ricotta, mascarpone, half the Parmesan, the egg and the cream. Season with salt and pepper.	4	Cook the pasta (see recipe 4). Drain, then allow to cool on a baking sheet. ➤

		FILLING
5	Butter a casserole dish. Fill a pastry bag with the ricotta filling and stuff the pasta, and then insert a few diced mushrooms into each lumaconi. Arrange the filled pasta in the casserole dish.	This ricotta and mascarpone–based filling is very creamy and replaces béchamel. It can be diluted as desired with a little cream.

| 6 | Sprinkle the remaining Parmesan on top of the filled pasta and dot with butter. Bake for about 20 minutes, until the top is well browned. Serve hot or warm. | **VARIATION**
❊
Prepare this recipe using fried speck or prosciutto and seasonal vegetables.
DELUXE VARIATION
❊
Add thin strips of black truffle before baking in the oven. |

VEAL RAGOUT TIMBALE

❖ SERVES: 6 • PREPARATION: 40 MINUTES • COOKING: 1 HOUR 30 MINUTES ❖

1 black truffle, canned or fresh
10½ ounces (300 g) ziti or bucatini (long tube pasta)
2½ tablespoons (37 ml) softened butter
¾ cup (175 ml) fresh bread crumbs

1 egg, beaten
1 pound (500 g) veal ragout (see recipe 47)
2 cups (500 ml) thin béchamel sauce
⅜ cup (90 ml) grated Parmesan
Salt and ground pepper, to taste

PRELIMINARY:
Slice the truffle into strips. Preheat the oven to 350°F (180°C).

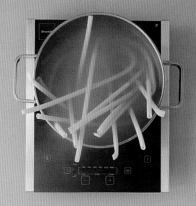

1 2
3 4

1	Boil the pasta in a large amount of salted water (see recipe 4).	2	Drain once the pasta is al dente and dress with a drizzle of olive oil. Arrange it on a baking sheet.	
3	Butter a 6-cup (1.5 L) ovenproof mold, dust with bread crumbs, brush with the egg and dust again with bread crumbs. Remove any excess.	4	Dress the pasta with the ragout, béchamel, ¼ cup (60 ml) Parmesan and the truffle.	➤

| 5 | Fill the mold with the pasta and ragout. Tamp down slightly and sprinkle the Parmesan combined with a couple of tablespoons of bread crumbs. Cover with buttered parchment paper. Bake for 45 minutes, removing the parchment paper for the last 5 minutes so the top is well browned. | **OPTION**
❀
Timbale makes quite an impact on the table, and its crust is delicious! Instead of a mold, you can use a round baking dish to prepare this recipe.

NOTE
❀
The truffle is optional, but it offers an exquisitely scented note! |

| 6 | Allow the timbale to rest for 5 minutes before turning it out onto a large plate. Serve it hot, sliced. | **RAGOUT VARIATION**
❊
Prepare this timbale with ragout made from different meats (beef, lamb, duck, pigeon, etc.) and with seasonal vegetables. |

SALADS

6

SOUTHERN PASTA SALAD

❖ SERVES: 4 • PREPARATION: 20 MINUTES • COOKING: 15 MINUTES ❖

2 tablespoons (30 ml) capers in brine
10½ ounces (300 g) canned tuna in olive oil
1¾ ounces (50 g) black olives
1¾ ounces (50 g) green olives
1 bunch fresh basil
½ bunch fresh parsley

4 tablespoons (60 ml) olive oil
2 tablespoons (30 ml) dried oregano
5 ounces (150 g) oven-roasted tomatoes
  (see recipe 7), or 3½ ounces (100 g)
  sun-dried tomatoes in olive oil
14 ounces (400 g) organetti or penne

PRELIMINARY:
Quickly rinse the capers under running water. They will help salt the dish. Drain the tuna and flake it with a fork.

1 2
3 4

1	Pit the olives and chop with the capers. Finely chop the fresh herbs. Assemble everything in a bowl.	2	Add the olive oil, oregano, tuna and oven-roasted tomatoes to the olives and capers.
3	Cook the pasta and drain when it's al dente (see recipe 4). Strain it and quickly run it under cold water to stop the cooking. Arrange it on a baking sheet and oil until it doesn't stick together.	4	Add the pasta to the tomato mixture and mix well. Taste to check the seasoning and adjust as needed. Serve at room temperature.

BAKED RIGATONI WITH PEPPERS

❧ **SERVES: 4:** • **PREPARATION: 20 MINUTES** • **COOKING: 40 MINUTES** ❧

2 tablespoons (30 ml) capers in brine
1¾ ounces (50 g) pitted black olives
2 yellow peppers
2 red peppers
8 anchovy fillets
¼ cup (60 ml) dry white wine

½ cup (125 ml) fresh bread crumbs
2 teaspoon (10 ml) dried oregano
Olive oil
14 ounces (400 g) penne or rigatoni
1 small bunch flat-leaf parsley
Salt and pepper, to taste

PRELIMINARY:
Rinse the capers under running water to remove some of the salt (do not remove the salt completely though, as the capers will help salt the dish). Preheat the oven to 350°F (180°C).

1 2
3 4

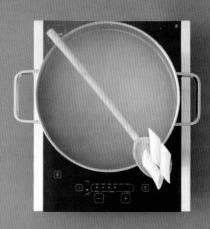

1	Coarsely chop the capers and the olives. Slice the peppers in half, clean and arrange on a baking sheet.	2	Stuff each pepper half with one anchovy fillet, sliced in half, and sprinkle the chopped capers and olives on top. Drizzle on the wine.
3	Mix the bread crumbs with the oregano, sprinkle on top, then drizzle on the olive oil. Bake until the peppers are tender, about 20 to 30 minutes. Leave to cool.	4	Meanwhile, cook the pasta and drain when al dente (see recipe 4). Strain it, then quickly run it under cold water. Arrange it on a baking sheet and oil so it won't stick together. ➤

| 5 | Slice the chilled peppers using a very sharp knife. | **ROASTED PEPPER PESTO VARIATION**
❋

Broil 5 red peppers. Peel. Blend with 2 ounces (60 g) roasted hazelnuts and 1 garlic clove. Add 2 to 3 tablespoons (30 to 45 ml) balsamic vinegar and 3 tablespoons (45 ml) bread crumbs, and dilute with ⅓ to ½ cup (75 to 125 ml) olive oil. Season with salt and pepper. |

Pennoni ai peperoni

| 6 | Combine the peppers with the pasta, drizzle olive oil over and sprinkle chopped parsley and pepper on top. Serve at room temperature. | **BAKED VEGETABLE VARIATION**
❋
Coarsely dice 1 eggplant, 1 red pepper, 1 carrot, 2 zucchini, 1 fennel bulb and 1 onion. Arrange in a single layer on a baking sheet and dress with olive oil, salt and pepper. Bake for 30 minutes at 400°F (200°C). Dress with 1 tablespoon (15 ml) balsamic vinegar and sprinkle chopped basil on top before serving. |

CONCHIGLIONI WITH CAPONATA

⇝ SERVES: 6 • PREPARATION: 1 HOUR • COOKING: 45 MINUTES ⇜

3 plum tomatoes
2 large eggplants
1 celery heart (reserve the leaves)
2 small onions
Olive oil, salt and pepper, to taste
4 tablespoons (60 ml) green olives

1 tablespoon (15 ml) capers, rinsed to
    remove salt
1 tablespoon (15 ml) raisins
1 tablespoon (15 ml) pine nuts
1 level tablespoon (15 ml) sugar
2 tablespoons (30 ml) red wine vinegar

1 pound (500 g) conchiglioni

PRELIMINARY:
Peel the tomatoes.

1	Dice the eggplant into ¾-inch (2 cm) cubes. Finely chop the celery. Seed the tomatoes and dice. Mince the onions.	2	Fry the diced eggplants in several batches in the olive oil, stirring frequently, until tender. Season with salt.
3	Boil the celery for 2 minutes in salted water.	4	In a large saucepan, cook the minced onions in a little olive oil for 2 minutes. ➤

5 6
7 8

5	Add the eggplants and celery to the onions, then add the olives, capers, raisins, pine nuts and tomatoes. Cook over low heat for 3 minutes, and then leave to cool.	6	Combine the sugar and the vinegar, and then pour this mixture into the pan. Cook, stirring, for several minutes over low heat.
7	Cook the pasta, stirring frequently. Drain the pasta when it's al dente (see recipe 4), quickly run it under cold running water and then arrange on a dish and oil lightly.	8	Stuff each shell with 1 tablespoon (15 ml) of cooled caponata.

| | Garnish with the celery leaves and serve at room temperature as an appetizer or as a main dish (allow 5 to 6 shells per person). | **ADVICE** ※ |
| 9 | | ☞ This is a light version of caponata, which is a traditional Sicilian dish. The caponata can be prepared 2 days ahead — it will only taste better! However, stuff the pasta just before serving. |

BROILED VEGETABLES PACCHERI

❧ **SERVES:** 4 (OR MAKES 30 HORS D'OEUVRES) • PREPARATION: 45 MINUTES • COOKING: 30 MINUTES ❧

1 or 2 eggplants
2 or 3 zucchini
4 tablespoons (60 ml) herb pesto
  (see recipe 9), diluted with a little olive oil

9 ounces (250 g) paccheri
About 30 stewed tomatoes (see recipe 7) or
  semi-dried tomatoes

Olive oil
Salt and pepper, to taste

1 2
3 4

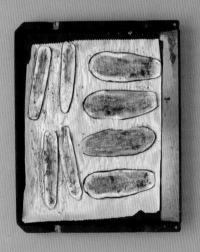

1	Slice the eggplant and zucchini ¼ inch (½ cm) thick.	2	Spread them out on a baking sheet lined with parchment paper. Brush the vegetable slices with the diluted herb pesto.	
3	Broil the vegetables until golden (they must not burn), then turn them over, brush again with pesto and broil until golden on the other side.	4	Cook the pasta and drain when it's al dente (see recipe 4). Quickly run it under cold running water, arrange it on a baking sheet and lightly oil.	➤

5	Slice the eggplant slices in half lengthwise. Place 1 zucchini slice on each half-slice of eggplant, then fold in half. Gently insert 1 zucchini-eggplant slice and 1 stewed tomato into each pacchero. Brush the paccheri lightly with herb pesto before serving.	**IN A SALAD** ❄ To make a pasta salad, use penne or similar short pasta. Use the herb pesto as a dressing and cut the broiled vegetables into strips. Mix the pasta, pesto and vegetables to combine, and garnish with the oven-roasted tomatoes.

6

Serve at room temperature as an appetizer or as part of a buffet. As an entrée, allow 4 paccheri per person and serve with an arugula salad.

VARIATION

Stuff the paccheri with broiled eggplant topped with tomato sauce and rolled with basil and a thin slice of mozzarella. Serve at room temperature or heat in a 350°F (180°C) oven for 10 minutes and serve warm.

CAPRESE SALAD

➤ **SERVES: 4 • PREPARATION: 30 MINUTES • COOKING: 15 MINUTES** ❖

1½ pounds (600 g) plum tomatoes
Salt and pepper, to taste
2 garlic cloves, chopped

Olive oil, to taste
14 ounces (400 g) conchiglie
1 cup (250 ml) basil pesto (see recipe 8)

9 ounces (250 g) buffalo mozzarella
 (preferably the small balls)

| 1 | Peel, seed and finely dice the tomatoes. Dress with the salt, garlic and olive oil. Allow to marinate for 30 minutes. | 2 | Cook the pasta and drain when it's al dente (see recipe 4), reserving ¼ cup (60 ml) of the liquid. Quickly run the pasta under cold running water to stop the cooking. Arrange on a baking sheet and oil so it does not stick together. |
| 3 | Dilute the pesto with the pasta cooking liquid. Remove the garlic from the tomatoes and dress the pasta with the pesto and the tomato mixture. | 4 | Season with pepper and serve with the mozzarella arranged on top. |

RUOTE WITH TOMATO-ALMOND PESTO

❧ SERVES: 4: • PREPARATION: 20 MINUTES • COOKING: 20 MINUTES ❧

12 ounces (350 g) ruote (wagon wheels) or
   other short pasta
1 garlic clove
5 plum tomatoes
6 to 8 tablespoons (90 to 120 ml) olive oil
1 tablespoon (15 ml) dried oregano

Salt and pepper, to taste
3½ ounces (100 g) whole blanched almonds
1 handful arugula, stems removed
3½ ounces (100 g) sun-dried tomatoes in oil
2 ounces (60 g) pecorino Romano (or
   Parmesan)

FIRST:

Cook the pasta so it's al dente (see recipe
4). Crush the garlic, de-germing it first if it
has begun to sprout.

1 2
3 4

1	Peel, seed and finely dice the plum tomatoes and mix with the olive oil, garlic clove and oregano. Season with salt and pepper.	2	Coarsely blend the almonds in a food processor. Chop the arugula and sun-dried tomatoes. Grate the cheese.
3	In a bowl, mix the diced tomatoes, sun-dried tomatoes, ⅔ of the almonds and the cheese.	4	Drain the pasta. Dress with a drizzle of olive oil, the tomato pesto and the arugula. Sprinkle the remaining almonds on top.

7

LASAGNA

LASAGNA PRIMAVERA

❧ SERVES: 4 • PREPARATION: 40 MINUTES • COOKING: 50 MINUTES ❧

1 bunch green asparagus
1 onion
2 zucchini
Olive oil, salt and pepper, taste
14 ounces (400 g) green peas, shelled

(about 3 cups/750 ml)
8 to 12 spinach lasagna sheets
 (see recipes 2 & 3)
1 pound (500 g) ricotta
½ cup (125 ml) heavy (36%) cream

2 tablespoons (30 ml) butter
9 ounces (250 g) crescenza or mozzarella
 (about 2 cups/500 ml)
¼ cup (60 ml) freshly grated Parmesan

1
4

2
5

3
6

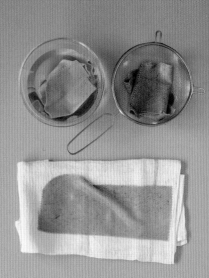

1	Slice the asparagus stems into rounds, setting the tips aside, and then dice the onions and the zucchini.	2	Cook each of these vegetables separately in a drizzle of olive oil (they should be cooked through but not soft). Season with salt.	3	Bring a pot of water to the boil, add salt and boil the asparagus tips for 2 to 3 minutes, then set aside.	
4	Cook the green peas in the asparagus water over low heat.	5	Boil the pasta sheets in the same water.	6	Remove pasta sheets with a small strainer or skimmer and drain on a dish towel.	➤

7 8
9 10

7	In a bowl, combine the ricotta and heavy cream. Season with pepper. Mix the cooked vegetables together in another bowl.	8	Butter a casserole dish, arrange a layer of lasagna sheets, a layer of ricotta and a layer of vegetables, then crumble some crescenza (or mozzarella) on top.
9	Repeat this step twice, finishing with the lasagna sheets and the ricotta cream on top, and then top with Parmesan and butter.	10	Fry the asparagus tips in a little butter. Set aside.

11	Bake in a 350°F (180°C) oven for about 20 minutes, until the top is well browned. Arrange the fried asparagus tips on top before serving.

VARIATION
❊

Replace the ricotta cream with béchamel sauce (see recipe 12) enhanced with Parmesan.

OPTION
❊

Instead of homemade lasagna, buy dried handmade egg lasagna or fresh vacuum-packed lasagna. Boil for 2 to 3 minutes then spread out on a dish towel in a single layer.

MEAT LASAGNA

VARIATION ON LASAGNA PRIMAVERA

❧ 1. Butter a casserole dish and pour in a little béchamel sauce (see recipe 12).

❧ 2. Arrange a layer of cooked pasta on top of the béchamel. Spread ⅓ of a batch of ragout (see recipe 11) and sprinkle grated Parmesan on top. Repeat 3 times.

❧ 3. Finish with a layer of pasta, then a layer of béchamel, then 2 tablespoons ragout. Dot with butter and sprinkle Parmesan on top. Bake for 20 to 30 minutes, until the top is well browned.

MUSHROOM LASAGNA

VARIATION ON LASAGNA PRIMAVERA

❧ 1. Butter a casserole dish and pour in a little béchamel sauce (see recipe 12).

❧ 2. Arrange a layer of cooked pasta, cover with béchamel and sprinkle 3½ ounces (100 g) fried mushrooms (see recipe 26) and a little Parmesan on top. Repeat 3 times.

❧ 3. Finish with a layer of pasta, then the remaining béchamel sauce and a few mushrooms. Dot with butter and sprinkle a little Parmesan on top. Bake for 20 to 30 minutes.

RADICCHIO LASAGNA

❖ SERVES: 6 • PREPARATION: 1 HOUR • COOKING: 30 MINUTES ❖

8 lasagna sheets (see recipe 2)
3½ ounces (100 g) Parmesan
1 pound (500 g) red chicory (radicchio)
  (preferably late, otherwise early)
2 shallots

2 tablespoons (30 ml) olive oil
½ cup (125 ml) red wine
Salt and pepper, to taste
1½ tablespoons (22 ml) butter
4 cups (1 L) béchamel sauce (see recipe 12)

PRELIMINARY:
Cook the lasagna sheets (see recipe 4).
Grate the Parmesan. Cut the radicchio into
quarters lengthwise and then wash it and
wring it dry.

1	Preheat the oven to 350°F (180°C). Peel and mince the shallots. Finely chop the radicchio.	2	Cook the shallots in the oil for 1 minute. Add the radicchio and cook for 3 minutes. Add the wine, allow to reduce and then season with salt and pepper.
3	Butter a casserole dish. Prepare 3 layers, alternating pasta sheets, béchamel sauce and radicchio and Parmesan. Finish with a layer of pasta, then the béchamel and lastly the radicchio tips.	4	Sprinkle the rest of the Parmesan over and dot with butter. Bake for about 20 minutes, until the top is nicely browned.

SQUASH LASAGNA

✦ **SERVES: 6 TO 8** • PREPARATION: 1 HOUR PLUS 40 MINUTES (FOR THE PASTA) • COOKING: 1 HOUR ✦

3½ pounds (1.5 kg) whole ambercup
squash, or about 4 cups (1 L) puree
1¾ ounces (50 g) amaretti biscuits (Italian
almond cookies)

3 ounces (80 g) mostarda di Cremona (fruit
sauce with mustard)
Freshly grated nutmeg, to taste
⅔ cup (150 ml) freshly grated Parmesan

Salt and pepper, to taste
6 lasagna sheets, cooked al dente (see recipe 2)
¼ cup (60 ml) butter

1 2
3 4

1	Slice the ambercup squash into large pieces, seed and steam until tender (20 to 40 minutes). Drain well.	2	Blend the amaretti biscuits in a food processor until finely ground. Next, blend the mostarda until pureed.
3	Blend the ambercup squash with an immersion blender or food processor until pureed (with the skin, if it is organic); you should obtain about 4 cups (1 L) of puree.	4	Add 4 pinches of nutmeg, the amaretti, the mostarda and 7 tablespoons (105 ml) Parmesan. Season with salt and pepper. ➢

5	Cut a sheet of lasagna in half. Spread a thin layer of the squash mixture on each half, leaving a ½-inch (1 cm) border. Roll the sheets and wrap each tightly in plastic wrap. Repeat this step until all the ingredients are used. Refrigerate for at least 1 hour.	**ADVICE:** ✻ ☛ It's best to cook the squash the day before, blend it and drain the puree in a strainer in the refrigerator to ensure all the moisture is removed. The filling should be thick and as easy as possible to compact. The ambercup squash can be replaced with butternut squash or your favorite winter squash.

| 6 | Butter a casserole dish. Cut each roll into 4 small sections and arrange in the casserole dish. Sprinkle the Parmesan on top and dot with butter and bake in a 350 °F (180 °C) oven for about 20 minutes. | **VARIATION** ❋
 Using the same filling, prepare a traditional layered lasagna or use with ravioli.
 SERVING ❋
 Serve 6 to 8 rolls per person as an entree or 2 per person as an appetizer. |

ARTICHOKE LASAGNA

SERVES: 6 TO 8 • PREPARATION: 1 HOUR 30 MINUTES • COOKING: 30 MINUTES

6 to 8 small purple artichokes
1 lemon
3 tablespoons (45 ml) olive oil
2 garlic cloves, peeled
½ cup (125 ml) dry white wine

1 tablespoon (15 ml) chopped parsley
Salt and pepper, to taste
6 lasagna sheets, cooked (see recipe 2)
1 egg white

**FOR THE CHEESE BÉCHAMEL
SAUCE:**

4 cups (1 L) béchamel sauce (see recipe 12)
9 ounces (250 g) Parmesan
3½ ounces (100 g) Gruyère
2 tablespoons (30 ml) butter

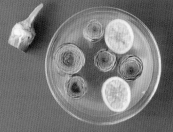

1 2
3 4

1	Remove the hardest artichoke leaves with a knife. Soak the artichokes in lemon juice to prevent them from browning.	2	Slice them in half, remove the choke, if there is one, then slice into strips.
3	Cook for 8 to 10 minutes over medium heat with the oil and garlic. Add the white wine, allow to reduce and then add the parsley. Season with salt and pepper. Add a little water as needed.	4	Grate the Parmesan and Gruyère. Mix all of the Gruyère and most of the Parmesan into the hot béchamel sauce. Allow to cool. ➤

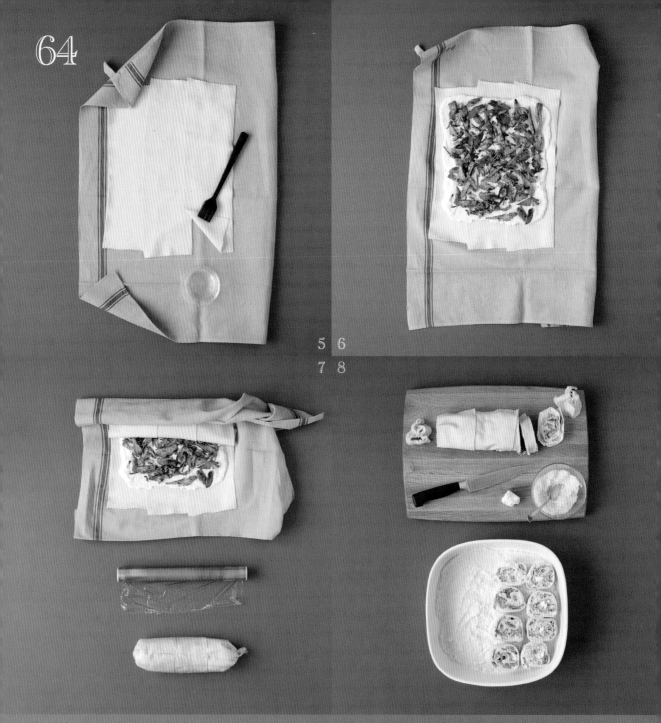

5 6
7 8

5	Place 3 lasagna sheets side by side with a 1-inch (2 cm) overlap; glue the edges together using the egg white.	6	Spread a layer of béchamel sauce about ¹⁄₁₆ inch (2 mm) thick and add half the artichokes.
7	Roll the lasagna in plastic wrap. Prepare a second lasagna using the remaining pasta sheets and artichokes and most of the béchamel. Reserve some béchamel for the topping. Refrigerate for 2 hours.	8	Butter a large baking dish and slice the lasagna into sections. Cover the bottom of the dish with béchamel and place the lasagna sections on top. Sprinkle the remaining Parmesan on top and dot with butter.

9	Bake in a 350°F (180°C) oven for 15 minutes, or until the top is a lovely golden color. Serve hot.	**OPTION** ❋ Replace the 3½ ounces (100 g) of Parmesan with 3½ ounces (100 g) of fontina.
NOTE ❋		**VARIATIONS** ❋
The lasagna must be refrigerated so the cheese cream can set. This makes it easier to slice the lasagna.		Replace the artichokes with mushrooms (see recipe 26). Using the same filling, prepare a traditional layered lasagna.

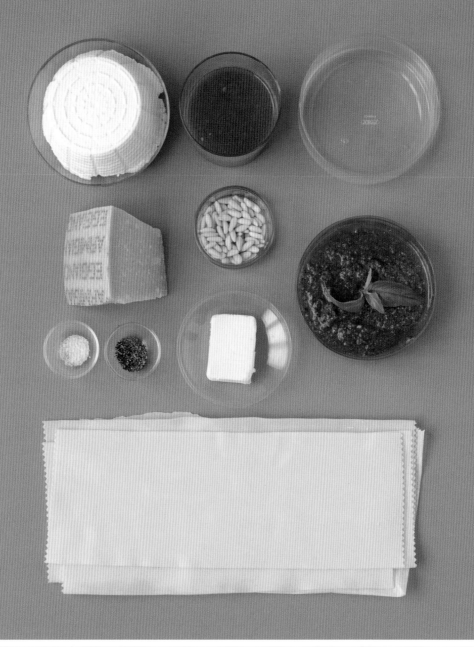

PESTO & RICOTTA LASAGNA LOAF

❧ SERVES: 6 • PREPARATION: 1 HOUR • COOKING: 30 MINUTES ❧

8 lasagna sheets, cooked (see recipe 2)
⅔ cup (150 ml) grated Parmesan
1 pound (500 g) ricotta or brocciu
  (about 2 cups/500 ml)
1 cup (250 ml) basil pesto (see recipe 8)
2 egg whites, lightly whisked

1½ tablespoons (22 ml) butter, melted
1¼ cup (310 ml) tomato coulis
¼ cup (60 ml) pine nuts, toasted
A few basil leaves, for garnishing

PRELIMINARY:
Butter a loaf pan. Slice the lasagna sheets
according to the size of the pan. Grate the
Parmesan.

1 2
3 4

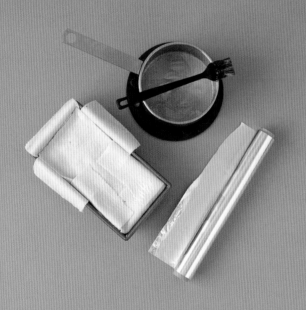

1	Mix the ricotta to obtain a uniform texture and then add the Parmesan, the pesto and the egg whites.	2	Line the bottom and the sides of the pan with pasta sheets. Cover with the filling. Prepare 4 layers, alternating pasta and filling.
3	Seal the lasagna loaf with the remaining sheets of pasta and brush with the melted butter. Cover with aluminum foil and bake in a 350°F (180°C) oven for 20 minutes.	4	Allow to rest for 10 minutes before turning the loaf out of the pan and slicing it. Serve hot or cold with the tomato coulis and accompanied by the toasted pine nuts.

RICOTTA & SPINACH CANNELLONI

❧ SERVES: 6 • PREPARATION: 1 HOUR • COOKING: 1 HOUR ❧

1½ pounds (600 g) fresh spinach, or
  10½ ounces (300 g) frozen
1 garlic clove
3 tablespoons (45 ml) butter
Freshly grated nutmeg, to taste
Salt and pepper, to taste

9 ounces (250 g) ricotta (about 1 cup/250 ml)
9 ounces (250 g) mascarpone (about
  1 cup/250 ml)
⅔ cup (150 ml) grated Parmesan
6 lasagna sheets, cooked (see recipe 2) or
  12 (4 × 6 inch/10 × 15 cm) sheets

½ cup (125 ml) heavy (36%) cream

PRELIMINARY:
Wash the spinach and remove the stems.
Peel the garlic and slice in half.

1 2
3 4

1	Steam the spinach until just wilted. Allow to cool, then drain by squeezing with your hands.	2	In a frying pan over low heat, dry the spinach in 2 tablespoons (30 ml) butter with the garlic. Add the nutmeg and season with salt.	
3	Allow the spinach to cool and chop with a knife (do not use a food processor, as the spinach will lose its flavor).	4	Mix the spinach with the ricotta, half the mascarpone and the Parmesan. Season with pepper and salt, as needed.	➢

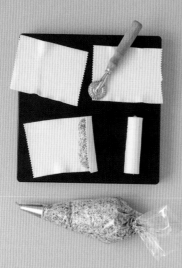

5 6
7 8

5	Slice the pasta sheets in half (you should obtain sheets that are about 4 × 6 inches/10 × 15 cm). Using a pastry bag, pipe spinach filling along the edge of each half-sheet and roll tightly to form cannelloni.	6	Butter a casserole dish and arrange the cannelloni accordingly.
7	Combine the heavy cream with the remaining mascarpone.	8	Top the cannelloni with the mascarpone cream and sprinkle Parmesan on top.

| 9 | Bake in a 400°F (200°C) oven for 20 minutes, until the top is golden. Serve hot. | **OPTION**
❈
Bake the cannelloni with 1¾ cups (425 ml) béchamel (see recipe 12) instead of the mascarpone cream.
VARIATION
❈
The cannelloni can be filled with ragout (see recipe 11) mixed with a little béchamel or with a ricotta-pesto mixture (see recipes 8, 9 and 10). |

STUFFED PASTA

8

SEA BASS RAVIOLI WITH LEEK CREAM

✦ SERVES: 6 • PREPARATION: 1 HOUR • COOKING: 15 MINUTES ✦

¼ cup (60 ml) butter
1 sprig rosemary
2 medium-sized leeks
1 small shallot
1 small bunch fresh parsley

10½ ounces (300 g) skinless sea bass fillets
    or monkfish fillets or raw shrimp
Salt and pepper, to taste
¼ cup (60 ml) olive oil
2 tablespoons dry white wine

Zest of 1 lemon
1¾ cups (425 ml) vegetable stock
1 pound (450 g) black pasta (see recipe 3)

1	Melt the butter over low heat with the rosemary. Turn the heat off and allow it to steep.	2	Wash the leeks and cut into rounds. Mince the shallot and chop the parsley. Dice the bass.	3	Cook the shallot in 2 table-spoons (30 ml) oil. Add the bass, cook for 30 seconds, and add the wine and allow it to reduce. Season with salt.
4	Move the bass to a bowl and flake with a fork. Add the parsley and lemon zest. Adjust the seasoning, if needed.	5	Lightly fry the leeks in the rest of the oil, then add the stock and cook for 10 minutes, covered.	6	Blend leeks with a blender or food processor until creamy. Add stock as needed."	➤

7 8
9 10

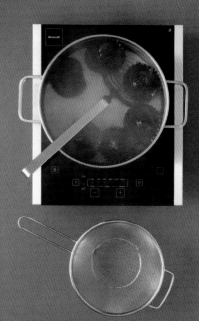

7	Roll out the pasta as you make the ravioli to prevent the dough from drying out. The dough should be about 1⁄16 inch (2 mm) thick.	8	Using 2 spoons, arrange small piles of filling at 2-inch (5 cm) intervals down the center of the rolled-out pasta sheet.
9	Cover with a second sheet of rolled-out pasta. Using your fingers, tamp down around the filling to remove any air and press the sheets of pasta together to seal. Cut out the ravioli.	10	Cook the ravioli for about 3 minutes in simmering salted water, and drain using a skimmer and strainer (so as not to break the cooked pasta).

11   Gently mix the ravioli with the heated rosemary-flavored butter and serve on a bed of hot leek cream.

TIP
※

You can precook the ravioli by simmering for 2 minutes and then combining with the flavored butter. To serve, arrange on a baking tray, cover with aluminum foil and heat in a 300 °F (150 °C) oven for 10 minutes.

STORAGE
※

Serve the ravioli as soon as possible (because of the fresh eggs and the filling, which will be saturating the pasta). They can be kept side by side, not stacked on top of each other, on a tray between 2 dish towels in the refrigerator for 24 hours. Otherwise, freeze them on a tray and store them in a bag once they are frozen. If the pasta is very thin, it may be better to precook the ravioli and butter it before freezing.

PECORINO & CITRUS FRUIT TORTELLI

VARIATION ON SEA BASS RAVIOLI WITH LEEK CREAM

✎1. Grate 7 ounces (200 g) pecorino and 5 ounces (150 g) Parmesan.

✎ 2. Mix with 5 ounces (150 g) ricotta (about ⅔ cup/ 150 ml), the zest from ½ an orange and ½ a lemon, 1 egg and a little salt and pepper. Refrigerate for 30 minutes.

✎ 3. Roll out a batch of light whole wheat dough (see recipe 3), and prepare the ravioli. Cook, then drain.

✎ 4. Combine with melted butter that you've flavored with the zest from the other ½ of orange and the other ½ of lemon.

PISTACHIO & ARUGULA RAVIOLI

VARIATION ON SEA BASS RAVIOLI WITH LEEK CREAM

✦ 1. Combine 1 cup (250 ml) pistachio and arugula pesto (see recipe 10) with 3½ ounces (100 g) ricotta or brocciu (about 7 tablespoons/105 ml).

✦ 2. Roll out a batch of Kamut dough (see recipe 3).

✦ 3. Prepare the ravioli, cook and barely drain.

✦ 4. Melt ¼ cup (60 ml) butter with a handful of arugula.

✦ 5. Gently mix the ravioli with the butter, sprinkle a little Parmesan on top and garnish with pistachios.

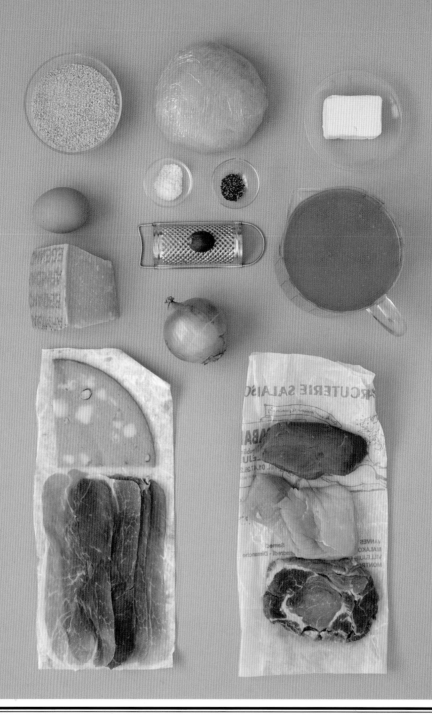

REGGIO EMILIA CAPPELLETTI

❖ SERVES: 6 • PREPARATION: 1 HOUR • COOKING: 3 MINUTES ❖

1 onion
10½ ounces (300 g) lean meats (such as 3½ ounces/100 g each of beef, veal and pork)
1¾ ounces (50 g) prosciutto
1¾ ounces (50 g) mortadella

2 tablespoons (30 ml) butter
¾ to 1 cup (50 to 60 g) fresh bread crumbs
Freshly grated nutmeg, salt and pepper, to taste
1 cup (250 ml) Parmesan, preferably aged 30 months

1 small egg, beaten
1 pound (450 g) pasta made with 2½ cups (625 ml) flour and 3 eggs (see recipe 2)
8 cups (2 L) beef or chicken broth

1 2
3 4

1	Mince the onion. Finely dice the meat. Chop the prosciutto and the mortadella.	2	Lightly brown the onion in the butter over low heat. Add the meats and cold cuts, and brown until golden. Season with salt and pepper.
3	Using a knife or food chopper, finely chop the meat mixture.	4	Toast the bread crumbs with a little nutmeg until golden. ➤

5 6
7 8

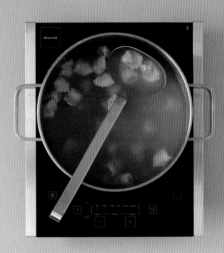

| 5 | Gradually mix the meat, ⅔ cup (150 ml) Parmesan, egg and bread crumbs; the filling should be thick and easily compacted. | 6 | Roll out the pasta so it's 1/16 inch (2 mm) thick (see recipe 2). Cut out 1-inch (3 cm) squares, place a knob of filling in the center of each, fold the pasta over to form a triangle and tamp around the filling. |
| 7 | Pinch the pasta to close around the filling, and fold two corners over your index finger until they touch to form the cappelletti. | 8 | Bring the broth to a simmer and cook the cappelletti for about 3 minutes. |

| 9 | Serve the cappelletti in the broth, with the rest of the grated Parmesan on the side. | **NOTE**

☞ In Emilia, a region of northern Italy, cappelletti are served at Christmas with capon broth, but they can also be eaten like traditional pasta, simply dressed with melted butter and Parmesan. |

ZUCCHINI DAISIES

❦ **SERVES: 6** • **PREPARATION: 40 MINUTES** • **COOKING: 15 MINUTES** ❦

2 or 3 zucchini
9 ounces (250 g) ricotta (about 1 cup/250 ml)
3½ ounces (100 g) fresh goat cheese
2 egg yolks
⅔ cup (150 ml) grated Parmesan
5 ounces (150 g) taleggio

2 tablespoons (30 ml) olive oil
1 garlic clove, peeled, halved and de-germed
  if it has begun to sprout
½ cup (125 ml) vegetable stock
1 pound (450 g) saffron pasta (see recipe 3)
3 tablespoons (45 ml) butter

1 small bunch fresh parsley
Salt and pepper, to taste

PRELIMINARY:
Finely dice the zucchini.

1 2
3 4

1	Mix the ricotta with the goat cheese, egg yolks and Parmesan. Remove the rind from the taleggio, discard it and finely dice the cheese.	2	Cook the zucchini for 5 minutes in the oil with the garlic. Season with salt.	
3	Reserve one-third of the zucchini for garnishing. Cook the rest of it in the stock for 5 minutes, then blend with an immersion blender or in a food processor.	4	Roll out the pasta and, using a pastry bag, pipe knobs of filling onto it. Place a piece of taleggio on top of each knob and cover with another sheet of rolled-out pasta. Cut out daisies with a cookie cutter.	➤

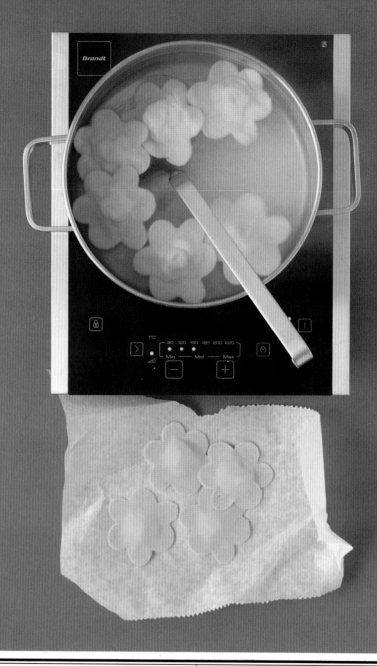

5	Cook the daisies in simmering salted water for about 3 minutes. Drain with a skimmer and strainer (to avoid breaking the cooked pasta). Meanwhile, melt the butter.	**VARIATION** ❀ Replace the saffron pasta with egg yolk pasta: combine 2½ cups (625 ml) flour, 10 egg yolks and a pinch of salt. To be eaten in small doses!

| 6 | Gently mix the daisies and the butter. When ready to serve, pour a little hot zucchini cream into the bottom of each plate, then add the daisies. Sprinkle the diced zucchini and a little Parmesan on top. | **PORCINI VARIATION**
❊
Replace the zucchini with porcini (fresh or frozen) cooked in olive oil, garlic and rosemary. Season with salt and pepper. |

BEEF & ESCAROLE TORTELLONI

❖ SERVES: 6 • PREPARATION: 40 MINUTES • COOKING: 30 MINUTES ❖

1 pound (450 g) pasta made with 2½ cups
  (625 ml) flour and 3 eggs (see recipe 2)
FOR THE FILLING:
1 escarole heart, or 1 bunch spinach (about 12
  ounces/350 g)
1 garlic clove, peeled

10½ ounces (300 g) cooked stewing beef
1 egg
⅓ cup (75 ml) grated Parmesan, preferably
  aged 30 months
Freshly grated nutmeg, salt and pepper,
  to taste

FOR THE DRESSING:
¼ cup (60 ml) butter
10 sage leaves
⅓ cup (75 ml) grated Parmesan
PRELIMINARY:
Wash, dry and coarsely chop the escarole.

1 2
3 4

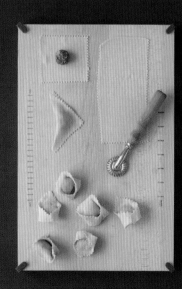

1	Heat a little oil in a frying pan, add the garlic and then, working in several batches, cook the escarole until tender. Season with salt and pepper.	2	Remove any fat from the beef and finely chop the meat. Chop the cooked escarole.	
3	Mix the meat and escarole then mix in the egg and Parmesan and season with nutmeg, salt and pepper.	4	Roll out the pasta and cut into 3-inch (8 cm) squares. Arrange a spoonful of filling in the center of each square. Fold the pasta over, join two ends and stick them together by pressing.	➢

5	Cook the tortelloni for 3 minutes in simmering salted water. Drain using a skimmer and strainer (to avoid breaking the cooked pasta).	**PREPARING THE TORTELLONI** ❊ Form a triangle when you fold the stuffed pasta over, and seal the edges by pressing with your fingers. Hold the triangle in one hand and join the two ends by pressing them between your index finger and thumb; there should be a space between the joined ends and the stuffed part of the tortellone.

6	Season the tortelloni with a melted sage-flavored butter (see recipe 76), and sprinkle Parmesan on top.

VARIATION
❋

Prepare agnolotti (square-shaped pasta typical of Italy's Piedmont region) using a filling of braised beef cooked with onions, pancetta and dry white wine that is mixed with Parmesan and nutmeg and dressed with meat juice or butter and Parmesan.

SWISS CHARD & SPINACH TORTELLI

⤞ SERVES: 6 • PREPARATION: 1 HOUR • COOKING: 30 MINUTES ⤝

14 ounces (400 g) green part of Swiss chard
14 ounces (400 g) spinach
7½ ounces (210 g) Parmesan
¼ cup (60 ml) butter

1 onion, chopped
3 tablespoons (45 ml) olive oil
1¾ ounces (50 g) bacon, diced (optional)
Salt and pepper, to taste

Freshly grated nutmeg, to taste
5 ounces (150 g) ricotta (about ⅔ cup/150 ml)
1 pound (450 g) chestnut pasta (see recipe 3)
1 garlic clove, halved

1	Steam the chard and the spinach for 4 minutes. Grate 5 ounces (150 g) of Parmesan (you should obtain about 1 cup/250 ml) and set aside. Melt the butter and set aside.	2	Drain the chard, allow to cool, then finely chop with a knife (do not use a food processor because the texture may not be the same).	
3	Cook the onion in 2 tablespoons (30 ml) oil over low heat for 3 minutes. Add the bacon and cook until golden.	4	Add the spinach and chard and cook over low heat until dry. Season with salt, pepper and nutmeg.	➤

5 6
7 8

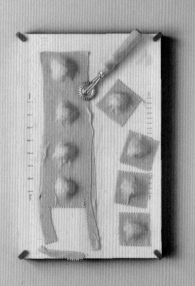

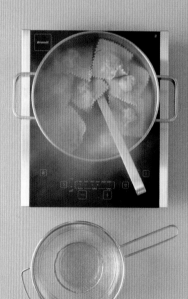

5	In a bowl, mix the spinach-chard mixture with the ricotta and grated Parmesan. Check the seasoning and adjust as needed.	6	Roll out a sheet of pasta to ¹⁄₁₆ inch (2 mm) thick and, using 2 spoons, drop little piles of filling at 2-inch (5 cm) intervals down the center of the pasta sheet.
7	Cover with a second sheet of rolled-out pasta. Using your fingers, tamp around the filling to remove any air and press the sheets of pasta together to seal. Cut out the tortelli.	8	Cook the tortelli for approximately 3 minutes in simmering salted water. Drain using a skimmer and strainer (to avoid breaking the pasta).

9 Gently mix the tortelli with the melted butter and serve with Parmesan shavings.

SQUASH TORTELLI
❋

Prepare an ambercup squash filling (see recipe 63). The filling must be thick, so drain the squash well by preparing it the day before and leaving the puree in a strainer in the refrigerator.

ARTICHOKE TORTELLI
❋

Cook the artichokes as indicated in recipe 64, finely chop them and then mix with 1 pureed potato and some Parmesan. Replace the chestnut pasta with a basic one made with 2½ cups (625 ml) flour and 3 eggs.

BEET HALF-MOONS

❖ **SERVES: 6 • PREPARATION: 1 HOUR • COOKING: 10 MINUTES** ❖

1 pound (450 g) pasta made with 2½ cups
(625 ml) flour and 3 eggs (see recipe 2)

FOR THE FILLING:
1 pound (400 g) beets, cooked
3½ ounces (100 g) onions
1½ tablespoons (22 ml) butter

1 russet or baking potato, cooked
1 egg
Salt and pepper, to tast

FOR THE DRESSING:
6 tablespoons (90 ml) butter, melted
2 ounces (60 g) Parmesan or aged Montasio

3 tablespoons (45 ml) poppy seeds

PRELIMINARY:
Peel the beets and blend in a food processor
or blender until pureed. Chop the onion.

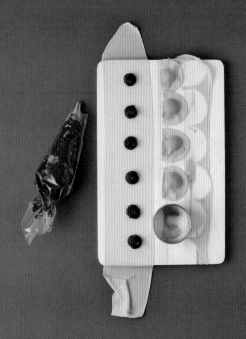

1	Cook the onions in the butter over low heat for 5 minutes. Add the beets and cook, stirring, for 2 minutes. Transfer to a bowl and allow to cool.	2	Mash the potato and add it and the egg to the cooled beet mixture. Mix thoroughly and season generously with salt and pepper.
3	Roll out the pasta so it's ¹⁄₁₆ inch (2 mm) thick and cut out circles between 2½ and 3 inches (6 and 8 cm) in diameter. Using a pastry bag, pipe a little filling in the center of each circle, and fold in half to form the half-moons. Press together to seal.	4	Cook in salted simmering water and dress with melted butter. Serve with Parmesan and poppy seeds sprinkled on top.

GNOCCHI

9

POTATO GNOCCHI

❧ **SERVES: 6 • PREPARATION: 30 MINUTES • COOKING: A FEW MINUTES** ❧

2¼ pounds (1 kg) potatoes
2¼ cups (560 ml) all purpose flour,
  approximately
1 egg

2 pinches salt
2 pinches freshly grated nutmeg

PRELIMINARY:
Wash the potatoes and steam or boil in simmering salted water for about 40 minutes. Remove the skins.

1 2
3 4

1	Working on a floured surface, mash the potato until pureed, then allow to cool.	2	Flour your hands, form a well in the puree and pour ¾ of the flour, along with the egg, salt and nutmeg, into the center of the well.	
3	Mix, moving from the center to the outer edge of the well. Incorporate the remaining flour as needed: the mixture must be supple and uniform.	4	Using floured hands, make ½-inch (1.5 cm) thick rolls, then slice into ¾-inch (2 cm) sections.	➢

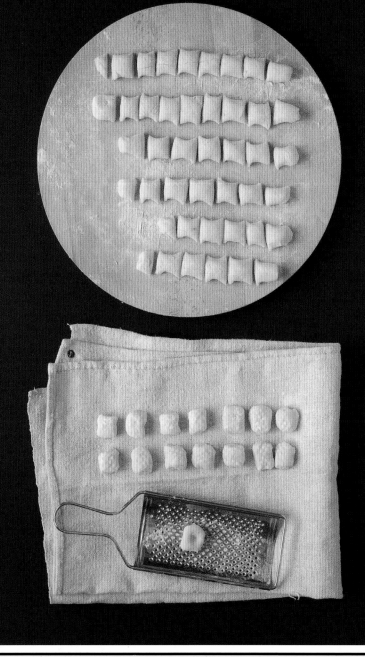

5	Place the gnocchi on a floured grater, press down on each with the tip of your finger and then arrange on a lightly floured dish towel.	### ADVICE ❄️ ☞ Do not overcook the potatoes, or they will absorb too much flour. Use as little flour as possible so the gnocchi remain soft. Do not blend the puree in a food processor, or it will turn into glue!

| 6 | Bring a large amount of salted water to the boil. Cook the gnocchi in 2 batches, removing them with a skimmer as soon as they rise to the surface. Arrange them on a buttered dish, and dress with the sauce of your choice (see recipes 76, 77, 78 and 79). To reheat, bake in a 400°F (200°C) oven for 10 minutes, until the tops are golden. | **TIP**
☞ Do not prepare gnocchi too far in advance (4 hours maximum), or they will become sticky and mushy. Cook any leftovers and refrigerate in an oiled dish; boil to reheat, but do not keep longer than 24 hours. |

GNOCCHI WITH BUTTER & SAGE

❖ **SERVES: 6 • PREPARATION: 5 MINUTES** ❖

✦ 1. Melt 7 tablespoons (105 ml) butter over low heat with a small bunch of whole sage leaves (or slice the leaves into thin strips).

✦ 2. Pour over the gnocchi and gently mix. Sprinkle ⅔ cup (150 ml) freshly grated Parmesan and dust with ground cinnamon, if desired.

TOMATO & BASIL GNOCCHI

❖ **SERVES: 6 • PREPARATION: 10 MINUTES** ❖

⤙ 1. Melt ¼ cup (60 ml) butter in a saucepan over low heat.

⤙ 2. Pour the melted butter over freshly drained gnocchi and mix gently.

⤙ 3. Serve with tomato sauce (see recipes 5 and 6) and basil, and sprinkle ⅓ cup (75 ml) freshly grated Parmesan on top, or add 9 ounces (250 g) of diced or shredded buffalo mozzarella.

GNOCCHI WITH GORGONZOLA

❊ SERVES: 6 • PREPARATION: 10 MINUTES ❊

❧ 1. Heat 7 tablespoons (105 ml) heavy (36%) cream and 1½ tablespoons (22 ml) butter over low heat.
❧ 2. Add 7 ounces (200 g) creamy Gorgonzola (without the rind) and break up with a fork. Allow to melt.

❧ 3. Pour the sauce over the gnocchi and mix gently.
❧ 4. Sprinkle ¼ cup (60 ml) grated Parmesan on top and serve. You can also add speck or prosciutto, sliced into thin strips, and crushed walnuts.

GNOCCHI WITH MUSHROOMS

❖ **SERVES: 6 • PREPARATION: 15 MINUTES** ❖

❖ 1. Melt 3 tablespoons (45 ml) butter over low heat with 3 tablespoons (45 ml) grated Parmesan.
❖ 2. Pour the sauce over freshly drained gnocchi and mix gently.

❖ 3. Serve topped with 10½ ounces (300 g) mushrooms that you've fried (see recipe 26), and freshly grated Parmesan. If you wish, you can flavor the gnocchi with truffle shavings.

SEMOLINA GNOCCHI

❧ **SERVES: 6** • PREPARATION: 50 MINUTES • COOKING: 40 MINUTES ❧

4 cups (1 L) milk
1½ cups (375 ml) finely ground wheat
  semolina
¼ cup (60 ml) butter

Salt, to taste
3 ounces (80 g) Parmesan
2 egg yolks

2¼ cups (560 ml) tomato sauce (see recipes
  5 or 6)

1	Heat the milk in a saucepan. When it starts to boil, pour in the semolina, stirring with a whisk.	2	Add 1½ tablespoons (22 ml) butter and the salt. Leave the saucepan over the heat for 20 minutes, stirring continuously with a wooden spoon.
3	Remove from the heat, add 3 tablespoons (45 ml) butter and ⅓ cup (75 ml) grated Parmesan. Allow to cool before mixing in the egg yolks.	4	Turn the semolina out onto a sheet of damp parchment paper and spread to a ½-inch (1 cm) thickness using a spatula dipped in water. Allow to cool. ➤

			OPTION ❋
5	Using a small glass or a cookie cutter dipped in water, create 2- to 2½-inch (5 to 6 cm) disks. Place the gnocchi on a large buttered baking dish, ensuring they overlap slightly.		Children really enjoy this dish. They love to cut out the gnocchi and to taste them! Think about varying the shapes — hearts, squares, etc.

6

Dot with butter and sprinkle Parmesan on top. Bake for 20 minutes, until very golden. Serve with tomato sauce.

VARIATION
❋

Before spreading out the semolina, add 3½ ounces (100 g) cold cuts (such as prosciutto, speck or cooked ham), finely diced, or aged cheese.

SQUASH GNOCCHI

✦ SERVES: 4 • PREPARATION: 20 MINUTES • COOKING: 40 MINUTES ✦

2¼ pounds (1 kg) ambercup or other winter
  squash, or about 4 cups (1 L) puree, well
  drained
1 egg, separated
4 ounces (120 g) ricotta (about ½ cup/125 ml)

1¾ ounces (50 g) Parmesan
¾ cup (175 ml) flour, sifted
Salt and ground pepper, to taste
Freshly grated nutmeg, to taste

FOR THE DRESSING:
6 tablespoons (90 ml) butter
10 sage leaves
3 ounces (80 g) smoked ricotta
  (about ⅓ cup/75 ml) or Parmesan

1 2
3 4

1	Wash the squash, slice it in half and seed and coarsely chop it. Bake in the oven at 300°F (150°C), covered with aluminum foil, or steam. Cook until tender.	2	Lightly whisk the egg white. Blend the squash pulp in a food processor and mix in the egg yolk, ricotta, Parmesan and egg white. Gradually add the flour little by little. Season with salt, pepper and nutmeg.
3	Using 2 spoons, form dumplings (quenelles). Cook in simmering salted water and drain as soon as they rise to the surface.	4	Season the gnocchi with the melted sage-flavored butter and sprinkle the smoked ricotta or Parmesan on top.

RICOTTA & SPINACH GNOCCHI

❧ SERVES: 6 • PREPARATION: 40 MINUTES • COOKING: 20 MINUTES ❧

2 shallots
1½ cup (375 ml) cooked and drained spinach
  (see recipe 66)
6 tablespoons (90 ml) butter
Freshly grated nutmeg, to taste
Salt and ground pepper, to taste

1 pound (500 g) fresh ricotta or brocciu
  (about 2 cups/500 ml)
1 large egg (or 2 small)
⅔ cup (150 ml) freshly grated Parmesan
12 sage leaves
1 cup (250 ml) flour, approximately

PRELIMINARY:
Finely chop the shallots and the cooked
and drained spinach with a knife (a food
processor will affect the flavor).

1 2
3 4

1	Sweat the shallots for 5 minutes in 1½ table-spoons (22 ml) butter. Add the spinach and cook until dry. Flavor with grated nutmeg and season with salt and pepper.	2	Break up the ricotta with a fork. Mix with the egg, Parmesan and warm spinach.
3	Using 2 spoons, form dumplings (quenelles), adding a little extra flour if they're mushy. Plunge into lightly salted simmering water. Cook for 1 minute from the time they rise to the surface.	4	Remove the gnocchi from the water with a skimmer and drain. Dress with the melted sage-flavored butter (see recipe 76) and sprinkle grated Parmesan on top.

APPENDIXES

ITALIAN INGREDIENTS

TABLE OF CONTENTS

RECIPE INDEX

SUBJECT INDEX

ACKNOWLEDGMENTS

ITALIAN INGREDIENTS

AMARETTTI
Cookies made from bitter almonds. There are soft ones (from Sassello) and crunchy ones (from Saronno). They're used in dishes with winter squash and mostarda.

AMBERCUP SQUASH
Its taste resembles that of Italian squashes. Also try acorn squash and butternut squash.

ANCHOVY
Use anchovies packed in brine (salt water) in cooked dishes and anchovies packed in olive oil in salads and other cold dishes.

AROMATIC HERBS
Basil, flat-leaf parsley, rosemary, sage and oregano are the most common herbs in Italian cooking.

BACON
The most famous and delicious Italian bacon is lardo di Colonnata. It is aged in marble containers in Colonnata, near Carrara (Tuscany), with herbs and spices for at least six months. It is served finely sliced on warm bread, grilled or wrapped around an Italian bread stick. It melts in your mouth.

BASIL
This is the ultimate Italian herb, used mostly during the summer. It can be found in tomato sauce, pesto and many other dishes.

BLACK OLIVES
Choose Taggiasca (pronounced "tadjasca") olives from Liguria. They are sweet and firm. They're usually sold pitted and jarred in olive oil. If you cannot find Taggiasca olives, choose Gaeta olives, which are sold in brine, or Leccine, niçoises, Nyons or black Lucca olives.

BOTTARGA
Mullet eggs that have been dried and pressed into a pouch coated with beeswax or paraffin; also called botargo. Try thin slices marinated in olive oil; ideal on crostini with tomatoes, in a salad or grated on spaghetti with olive oil. There is also tuna roe bottarga, which is saltier and has a stronger flavor. Available at high-end specialty food stores and online.

BREAD CRUMBS
You can make your own bread crumbs by grating stale bread or blending stale bread and melba toast, preferably organic, in a food processor.

BURRATA
A cow's milk cheese typical of the Apulia region (the heel of Italy). Its outer shell is made of spun cheese (as is mozzarella), and it is filled with the same cheese mixed with cream. It must be eaten within 2 to 3 days and can be eaten on its own or in pasta dishes. Available at specialty food stores.

CANNED TOMATOES
Choose crushed tomatoes (100% tomatoes plus salt), preferably Italian ones.

CANNED TUNA
Choose tuna in a jar, so you can see the pieces, and in olive oil for the flavor. It complements pastas and salads. The belly and the marrow are the tastiest parts of the tuna.

CAPERS
Capers are a flavorful substitute for salt. The best are from the small islands around Sicily (Pantelleria, Salina and Lipari). Rinse under running water for a few minutes to remove some of the salt.

CAPONATA
A type of bittersweet stew, typical of Sicily, made from eggplant, tomatoes, celery and vinegar. It's served at room temperature as an entrée or as a side dish or dressing. Perfect on pasta salad!

CREAM
In Italy, light cream is used primarily in desserts and practically not at all in pasta sauces. Sour cream is non-existent. Instead, use heavy cream or whipping cream.

CRESCENZA, STRACCHINO AND CASATELLA
These fresh cheeses from northern Italy are soft, preservative-free and rich in lactic starter.

DRIED PASTAS
Short pastas go well with most sauces because the sauces adhere to them well. Spaghetti is indispensable with seafood. With meat ragout choose egg tagliatelle, definitely not spaghetti (the sauce doesn't adhere to it). Dried pastas are made from hard wheat and water. Choose handmade pastas: rough and porous, they absorb sauces and condiments better. Among manufactured pastas, choose those made using Trafile bronze-coated pasta dies.

EGGS
Choose organic medium-sized eggs.

FREGOLA
This small pasta is made of roasted hard wheat and is typical of Sardinia.

GARLIC
Always have some on hand! It's almost always used to cook with vegetables in olive oil, to flavor a dish. Be careful not to burn it.

GORGONZOLA
A soft and creamy veined cheese, Gorgonzola is originally from Lombardy (northern Italy). It can be melted with cream or milk to make a sauce for pasta or gnocchi. It's also available combined with mascarpone, which is an ideal spread.

GREEN OLIVES
Choose large Cergnola, picholine or Lucca olives.

MASCARPONE
A cream-based dairy product, mascarpone is delicate and smooth. It has the texture of very thick cream, and it is an indispensable ingredient for tiramisu. I use it combined with ricotta and spinach.

MOSTARDA
Spicy seasoning made of candied fruit flavored with mustard. The most common is mostarda di Cremona. I use it with ambercup squash.

MOZZARELLA
There are 2 types: cow (fiordilatte), which is typical of Apulia (southwestern Italy), and the more flavorful buffalo, also called mozzarella di Campania. Eat it soon after buying, and store it in its own liquid and serve at room temperature. It is sold in different shapes, including balls and braids.

OLIVE OIL
Choose first cold-press extra virgin olive oil from Italy. In general, the oil from the north is sweeter, while the oil from the center and south is fruitier. When frying, you can heat olive oil up to a temperature of 350°F (180°C), or use peanut or grapeseed oil instead.

ORECCHIETTE
A hard wheat pasta that is typical of Apulia, in southeastern Italy, and is in the shape of little ears, as the Italian name suggests.

OREGANO
Aromatic herb that I use dried. Choose oregano from southern Italy or organic oregano. I mostly use it in the summer with tomatoes, eggplants and peppers.

PANCETTA
A cured or smoked (affumicata) bacon that is diced for use with pasta. It can replace guanciale (pork cheeks), which is hard to find outside of Italy, in amatriciana and carbonara pastas.

PARMESAN
Parmigiano-Reggiano has Protected Designation of Origin status, or PDO. When made outside the designated Italian regions, it is called Parmesan. It is the indispensable cheese for pasta. Use authentic Parmigiano-Reggiano if you can, and buy it in chunks, never already grated and in a bag (the taste is not the same). Parmigiano-Reggiano is more flavorful when aged more than 12 months, so choose varieties that have been aged for 18, 24, 30 or more months.

PECORINO
Made from ewe's milk, pecorino Romano, a dry cheese, is ideal for grating on pasta. Frequently used in south-central Italy instead of Parmigiano-Reggiano. Pecorino is sweeter when fresh, and the flavor gets saltier as it ages.

PEPPER
Choose whole peppercorns and grind as needed. Use sparingly and preferably ground right over the dish, when ready to serve. In Italy, not all dishes are systematically seasoned with pepper.

PINE NUTS
Crunchy and delicious. It is better to toast them before use. They are often used with raisins in Venetian, Neapolitan and Sicilian recipes and in basil pesto in Liguria.

PISTACHIOS
The most famous are those from Bronte in Sicily. Choose blanched pistachios (unsalted); otherwise blanch them yourself, by boiling them for 2 minutes and then removing the thin skin that covers them.

PROVOLA
Made from cow's milk, provola is a spun cheese, like mozzarella. It's available plain or smoked, which is a more interesting version. I especially like it in pastas au gratin.

RAGOUT
The name means a sauce based on ingredients that are chopped or cut into small pieces (ragout alla bolognese, meat ragout and the like).

RAW HAM
Choose ham from Parma or San Daniele, and ask your butcher to slice it finely without the rind. The ham should have at least ½ inch (1 cm) of fat. The more aged the ham is, the better it tastes. Parma and San Daniele hams only contain pork and salt — no additives.

RICOTTA
A dairy product made from cow, ewe or buffalo milk. It is made by cooking the milk whey twice, hence the name, which means "re-cooked." A delicate cheese, it adds creaminess to pasta dishes. Handmade fresh ricotta is a real treat; otherwise use brocciu.

SALT
Choose unprocessed sea salt, which is rich in trace elements, and fleur de sel.

SMOKED RICOTTA
Very flavorful, it is ideal for coarsely grating on pasta and gnocchi.

SPECIAL PASTAS
Kamut, spelt . . . These pastas are sold in organic food stores. They have a higher nutritional value than wheat pastas and are easier to digest.

SPECK
A mountain ham that is smoked and de-boned. It's from Alto Adige in northern Italy.

SPICES
Saffron, nutmeg and cloves are the most widely used spices in Italian cooking. Nutmeg is indispensable with spinach and in béchamel sauce. Choose to freshly grate whole nutmeg and avoid ground nutmeg, which quickly loses its flavor.

STOCK
Instead of a homemade stock you can use organic bouillon cubes (which don't have flavor enhancers). They're available in large supermarkets and organic food stores.

SUN-DRIED TOMATOES
The good ones are not too salty nor too vinegary but sweet and soft. Those that come from Apulia and Sicily are bursting with sunshine! Ideal for making pesto. Semi-dried tomatoes are softer and sweeter.

TALEGGIO
A tasty soft cheese, taleggio is originally from Lombardy. Try it plain or melted as a ravioli filling, on a crostino or in risotto.

TABLE OF CONTENTS

1
THE BASICS

2
EXPRESS

3
VEGETABLES

4
SEAFOOD & FISH

5

MEATS

6

SALADS

7

LASAGNA

8

STUFFED PASTA

9

GNOCCHI

RECIPE INDEX

SUBJECT INDEX

HARD WHEAT PASTAS

EGG PASTAS

SPECIAL PASTAS

ACKNOWLEDGMENTS

Grazie mille to the entire gourmet team of *Pasta Basics*: I had a great time with you!
A big thank you to Pierre Javelle for his beautiful photos, his kindness,
his great cooking and his collaboration.

To Marie Mersier, for the shopping and the paint, and for being available!

To Ariadne Elisseeff, for her valuable help and sound advice at any time.

To Audrey Génin, for her collaboration and for coordinating everything.

To Marabout and to Rose-Marie Di Domenico, my editor.

To my friends Emmanuelle M. and Sandrine R., for their help and all the laughs.

To my family, who passed on a taste for the finer things, and to my daughter, Eva.

A very big thank you to all the press agents and the stores that provided the paint,
the dishes and all the utensils and accessories needed to put this book together.

And thank you to the family of Serafino Zani, for the beautiful saucepans.